# RECLAIM
# YOUR FAMILY
# FROM
# ADDICTION

# RECLAIM YOUR FAMILY FROM ADDICTION

## How Couples and Families Recover Love and Meaning

Craig Nakken

p

**■ HAZELDEN®**

INFORMATION & EDUCATIONAL SERVICES

Hazelden
Center City, Minnesota 55012-0176

1-800-328-0094
1-651-213-4590 (Fax)
www.hazelden.org

Library of Congress Cataloging-in-Publication Data
Nakken, Craig.
  Reclaim your family from addiction : how couples and families recover
love and meaning / Craig Nakken.
    p. cm.
  Includes bibliographical references and index.
  ISBN 1-56838-519-6
  1. Alcoholics—Family relationships. 2. Narcotic addicts—Family
relationships. 3. Alcoholics—Rehabilitation. 4. Narcotic addicts—
Rehabilitation. I. Title

HV5132 .N35 2000
362.29'13—dc21                                                     00-044955

AUTHOR'S NOTE
All the stories in this book are based on actual experiences. The
names and details have been changed to protect the privacy of the
people involved. In some cases, composites have been created.

EDITOR'S NOTE
The Twelve Steps are reprinted with the permission of Alcoholics
Anonymous World Services, Inc. (AAWS). Permission to reprint the
Twelve Steps does not mean that AAWS has reviewed or approved the
contents of this publication, or that AAWS necessarily agrees with the
views expressed herein. AA is a program of recovery from alcoholism
only—use of the Twelve Steps in connection with programs and activities which are patterned after AA, but which address other problems,
or in any other non-AA context, does not imply otherwise.

04 03 02 01 00   6 5 4 3 2 1

Cover design by Adrian Morgan
Interior design and typesetting by Spaulding & Kinne

The book is dedicated to our niece and goddaughter
Jennifer Lynn Overkamp
January 21, 1982 to May 29, 1998

Thank you, Jenny,
for teaching all who met you about the
importance of love, family, community,
for your values and the way you lived them.

# Contents

# Contents

# CONTENTS

## ✥ Part 4: Recovery ✥

*T*his book was started in my heart many years ago by people like Irene Whitney, John Siverson, and Terry Williams. Irene was my first counselor; she gave me hope where there had been none. John and Terry taught me about addiction and opened the door to the world of miracles. Terry, with his love for the recovering family, sparked a flame inside me that has never gone out. Mentors and friends like Merle Fossum, Rene Schwartz, Marilyn Mason, Marilyn Peterson and Norton Amour, Karen Johnson, Jim Jacobs, Glenice Anderson, Vern Wagner, Mary Froiland, Denise D'Aurora, Dave Walsh, Gail Hartman, and many more have helped me greatly in learning and working with the addictive family. To be blessed with such friends and colleagues is an honor.

The friends at Rutgers Summer School for Addiction Studies and at the Florida Summer School of Addiction Studies over the past decade and a half have allowed me to think and work on ideas in a climate of challenge and excellence in learning.

A special thanks to Ove and Lena Rosengren and Calle Fjellman for creating a way for me to return "home" to Sweden and to give to this home the gifts that have been given to me. For LG, Gunvor, Jennie and Kalle Persson, Mr. "William" (Börje) Dahl, and everyone on staff at Granhult Treatment Center in Ramsberg, Sweden, there are not words to express the thanks and awe I feel toward the most generous people I have ever met. At Granhult—within an environment of curiosity, laughter, fellowship, and challenge—I've been able to explore and articulate my thoughts and ideas. (For those of you who have never been there,

Ramsberg, Sweden, is the spiritual center of Sweden. It is a special place where family and friends mix and create renewal and hope.)

For Hazelden and the opportunities they've given me to touch people through words, thank you. For Nick Motu and Becky Post, thank you. Thank God for Richard Solly, my editor, who helped change thoughts and ideas into words with heart. And thank you for the laughter and fun we've had in doing it. (I know, I know, "more examples.")

Thanks to friends like Gene and Cathy Synder, Tom Piechel, and Cathy Seward, Karen Elliot and Joe Casey, who kept me from getting too crazy in my busyness—a little distant, but not too crazy. To dear special friends Sandy and Damian McElrath, thank you. A special thanks to Damian for planting the seed that got this book growing. To those who believe in complete defeat, thank you.

To my family and extended family, my mother and her twenty-six years of hope and sobriety, thank you for the healing we've done over the years.

To my wife, partner, and best friend, Janie, read the dedication to the first book—it still goes on.

But the main thanks for this book must be to the hundreds of clients and the recovering families that over the years have shown and taught me how the hells of addiction must be transformed into a renewal of connections and commitments to love and meaning.

# PART 1

## LOVE AND PRINCIPLES

# Introduction to Part 1

### Scene 1

It was after 6:00 P.M. when Ted Jensen arrived home, grumbling to himself about his boss. Ted was late, but still within the twenty-minute guideline he and his wife, Maggie, had agreed upon before one would have had to call. As he entered the house, Ted heard the sizzle and spit of water spilling out of a pan of potatoes into flickering yellow flames. David, their six-year-old, was sitting in the kitchen on "The Chair" as it had become known. An egg timer on the table showed three minutes left. Ted walked over to his son and rubbed his hand through his hair. "I'll talk to you soon," he said.

"She's in the bedroom," David hollered as his dad left the kitchen.

Ted walked upstairs where he found Maggie, bent over, whisk broom in hand, cleaning up the scattered remains of her favorite lamp. He stood still and quiet. This was not a time for him to talk about how grumpy he felt. "You're late!" she said gruffly.

Ted now had to choose. Does he complain and let her know that he, too, was having a bad day or does he try to be helpful?

At that moment, they both heard the egg timer go off downstairs. "I wish he could sit there till he graduates from high school," Maggie said. There was just enough humor and apology in her voice for them to share a brief smile.

"Yeah, I'm late, but within our twenty-minute limit," he said as he kissed her cheek. "Can I help?"

David suddenly appeared at the door. For a moment, Maggie and David stared at each other. "We don't play pirate in the house," she said to her son.

David knew how important the lamp was to his mother, but still he tried to defend himself: "But, it's winter outside."

"That's why we have jackets!" Ted said to let David know he was dealing with two parents and not just one. Ted walked over to his son and put his arm around his shoulder. "Honey, you finish up here. David and I will finish fixing supper."

"Thanks." Maggie felt calmer. "You help Dad, Mr. Pirate."

The entire family was finding a way to weather the crisis. Half an hour later, while sitting at the dinner table, David apologized: "I'm sorry, Mom. I didn't mean to break your lamp."

## Essence of Family

We start this part, and every part hereafter, with a scene from the Jensen family to illustrate particular principles. This scene represents a typical family at dinnertime. Working parents like Ted and Maggie often arrive home at the end of the day to face a set of tasks very different from the ones they manage at work. Though the family may have developed a system for picking up children at day care and making supper, annoying problems such as broken lamps can disrupt the routine. Family interaction isn't always fun. The Jensen family scene may seem familiar and simple, but underlying the routines are complex issues. That's because family isn't simple. Families are made up of a mixture of personalities and must deal with a wide array of tasks, emotions, hopes, values, struggles, and solutions.

The very makeup of a family today is not cut and dried. Besides the traditional two-parent families, there are blended families with children from different marriages, interracial families, adopted families, single-parent families, families with gay or lesbian parents, foster-parent families, families of origin, and the human family—our community. Additionally, families are not static. The individual family members constantly change, grow, and learn. This creates a unique composition and energy for each family. For example, one family may prefer to spend their Saturday afternoon at the local art museum and another at a baseball game. And let's not forget that families come together with a history. This means that, in addition to a family's immediate members, distant relatives from generations ago subtly shape and influence a family's spirit and rituals.

I recently attended a family reunion in the Midwest with more than two hundred relatives who shared a history started by two pioneers who homesteaded a hundred sixty acres of prairie in the 1800s. At the reunion, the family spirit that was set in motion long ago and that had been passed through four generations now seemed palpable, as real and nurturing to me as the cherry pies, conversations, balloons, and softball games. Among the laughter and chatter of children, aunts and uncles, grandmothers and grandfathers at the picnic tables, I heard a distant voice chant: *remember* the beginning, *remember* the past, *remember* the prairie. Like other families, my family feels a certain unity from our collective history. These experiences from the past, however, mean more than just a set of dates and facts. They teach us about the values and principles that our ancestors lived by—and that we live by today. Indeed, families need to foster and develop a strong principle-based life to maintain relationships and connections among themselves, if not to other generations and relatives. Principles and values are critical in shaping the family. Without them, the family will not thrive. To understand the Jensens, we must understand the nature of love itself, how Ted and Maggie like any couple began their lives together and eventually the lives of their children. This book is about love and families created by spiritual principles, called principles of betterment; families that are destroyed by alcoholism and addiction; and families that recover and realign themselves along spiritual principles and meaning.

# CHAPTER 1

# PRINCIPLES OF BETTERMENT

## Two Types of Love

*The principle task for every couple and family is to create and sustain love.* Love is the very blood of families. Two types of love are critical in shaping the direction and purpose of any couple or family: *formless love* and *created love*.

### Formless Love

Most people have experienced formless love at some time in their lives. It is instinctual love. We sometimes call it "chemistry," the "spark" or "click" that couples often feel when they first meet. Formless love is primarily a sensory experience. The quality of the relationship is determined by how it feels. If it feels good, you continue. If the first date doesn't feel right, you usually find a nice way to say thank you and good-bye.

Formless love is "blind" to the frailties and short-comings of the other, and it alone cannot shape a life or direction for the couple. However, it does contain the ingredients from which "true" love can emerge. If we compare formless love to an art, then it is the clay that the sculptor has yet to shape into something meaningful and formed. Formless love possesses the words to a poem that hasn't been structured into sentences and stanzas; it contains the colors, brushes, canvases, and beautiful emotional scenery, but these components haven't been formed or imagined into a new creative life of its own. In short, formless love, though brimming with desire and "chemistry," is without shape, principles, goals, or meaning. A couple can experience formless love for many years—an entire life in fact. It takes more than chemistry and sparks to create enduring love.

Struggling to sustain their ten-year marriage, a couple who were in their forties came to me for therapy. When I asked them to describe their early courtship, their eyes lit up. "It was wonderful," Karen said. "We would sit and dream together. He would listen to my stories, thoughts, hopes, and I'd look at him thinking he was the most handsome man I had ever seen. And he was." Richard blushed and added: "She was quite the dreamer, and they were good dreams. She gave words to things I'd always felt but couldn't articulate. She made me feel whole." As they talked about their early formless love, a strength and vitality enlivened each of them. However, desires, dreams, and good intentions alone cannot create a solid relationship.

Richard and Karen's love had remained formless for many years. It hadn't yet grown out of its infancy. This was their pain. They were haunted by unrealized dreams. Something more was needed. They had all the ingredients—the clay, words, colors—to create love and meaning, but they had not done so.

A set of skills, along with ingredients, are needed to shape love in a meaningful way. As faith without works is empty, so love without skills is also empty; that is, it remains formless. Defining love as a set of skills may not be very romantic, but skills are exactly what is needed in the long run to keep romance alive. Any couple who want to develop and deepen their love must acquire skills, acquire spiritual principles, and be willing to practice living by these principles until they become a natural part of everyday life.

Richard and Karen needed to move into the second and most important type of love: *created love*. Although the couple wanted an intimate relationship, they lacked skills to create true intimacy. They had simply never learned how to move a relationship to the next level: the level where couples create love that nourishes and sustains the relationship. Both had come from severely abusive families. Early in their marriage, Richard drank too much and once, during an argument, hit Karen. It was the only such incident in the marriage, but the violence sent both of them back into unresolved feelings from their youth. They couldn't get past this turbulent period of their marriage. My task as their therapist was to teach them the skills, developed from spiritual principles, that they needed to resolve issues and bring their marriage to the next level. The goal of recovery and therapy is simple: to return individuals to their humanity and their ethics, and in so doing restore their *ability to love* themselves and others and to create love in their relationships.

### Created Love

Created love is defined as formless love transformed. Created love is clay finally shaped by a sculptor into a beautiful piece of pottery; words meaningfully composed into stanzas and poems; colors brushed onto a canvas into something that has never before been seen. Created love is very much like an object of art—a spiritual art. It takes the energy and power of formless, instinctual love, and, without breaking its spirit, uses and turns its raw desires into skills, structures, discipline, and commitment.

In order to understand and create recovery, then, we must first understand love and the skills we use to demonstrate love on a daily basis. Love is difficult to discuss because the subject is so vast. All of us define and conceptualize love in slightly different ways. However, we would all agree that love is transformed from a formlessness into a creation when we use skills based on principles of betterment. (We'll discuss these spiritual principles on pages 42–52.)

Unlike formless love, created love has the power to resolve conflicts and bind individuals together into a force that produces growth and betterment for all involved. Created love is the highest and most developed form of love. It evolves from spiritual discipline and is guided by spiritual principles. Created love helps transform us from human beings to spiritual beings. Because active addicts and alcoholics refuse to abandon the sensations of the human world for the principles of a spiritual one, they are unable to experience the joys and refuge that can be found in created love. Rather, the sensations of the high are the addict's only sanctuary.

Created love works to bind together past, present, and future. It believes in a future and takes it into account. We act in loving ways not just to feel good, but because today's actions are tomorrow's foundation. In created love, fun and excitement naturally evolve into joy and contentment.

The creative and destructive aspects of our humanity are also connected in creative love. This type of love is neither unconditional nor conditional, but a blend of the two. We might describe created love as a paradox, as unconditional love with conditions attached to it. The I'll-love-you-no-matter-what-you-do attitude of unconditional love is romantic and unreasonable to assume in any family, let alone in an addictive family system. With this attitude, principles get sacrificed. However, conditional love, I'll-love-you-only-after-you've-met-certain-conditions, is unreasonable to expect of addicts and alcoholics. Addicts can rarely meet these conditions.

Created love combines conditions with an attitude of unconditional positive regard. It is a higher form of love. It states: "I'll always love you, and because of this I'll put conditions on you and me that must be met if love is to mean anything. These conditions or principles, such as respect, are more important than you or I. In order for us to grow in love, you and I must demonstrate these principles through our actions."

An example may be helpful. A few months back I watched a television interview of a mother caught in a horrible situation. Her son had told her he was going to murder someone. She couldn't stop him and the murder was committed. She ended up turning him in to the police and being the main witness against him in court. Although this woman could have lied to protect her son from the consequences of his behavior, that would have reduced her to being a coconspirator instead of a mother. She was in anguish. If convicted, her son could receive the death penalty. In an interview, she said: "I love him and I'll always love him, but there are more important things than him or me. What he did was wrong. The only way left for me to be truly his mother was to turn him in. I pray that he understands." What she did was the most loving thing she could have done for her son.

As a loved one gets sicker from addiction, family members often compromise their own principles and integrity. They may lie to employers, deceive other family members, or ignore threatening behavior. They do this in the name of love, but it is not love. It is the addictive process itself. Family members often compromise themselves by enabling irresponsible behavior. The honest spouse may often find himself in situations where he feels forced to lie about the condition of his spouse, betraying his own ethics and principles.

The family feels caught in a double bind. Do members act according to principles, such as honesty, that support love, or do they lie to protect the addicted family member? While they may believe they have to choose between the two, they can stay attached to both: their principles and the addict. This solution, based on created love, combines unconditional love with conditions or principles. Remember, the primary spiritual task of families is to create and sustain love.

## Principles of Betterment

Created love is conditional as far as it puts what's best for us ahead of what we want. In recovery this is often referred to as placing *principles before personalities*. Principles make love more dependable. They are the workhorses of love and drive a couple or family to meaningful relationships. When we live our lives according to the *principles of betterment,* love is created and spiritual growth occurs. Examples of principles for betterment include truth, love, and equality. These principles of betterment help us to see love as more than a set of fast-moving emotions and chemistry. Through these principles, love becomes tangible and can be transformed into a set of skills.

Principles of betterment also allow and teach us to surrender our egos, a skill that is needed to form intimate relationships. By repeatedly putting principles before personality, we gain control over our own egos. We learn that the principles of betterment are more important than any one of us.

If we put our egos before principles, on the other hand, we are saying we are more important than these principles. We abandon truth for a terrible, destructive illusion.

For more years than I care to remember, I acted in an unprincipled and unkind manner. As an addict, I stole, cheated, and for years was either doing something illegal or in the possession of something illegal. I was cruel to my family, my friends, and anyone who showed me any care, unless being with them meant I could secure more drugs. I chased after any sensations that might promise me moments of pleasure or a sense of power. Principles were sacrificed to that goal.

In recovery, I started spending time with people who believed in principles more than personalities, power, or pleasure. They told me to do small acts of respect. Near self-destruction and with no other real choice, I did what I was told and began asking others how their day was. I listened. I began showing up on time. If someone needed help, say moving furniture, I helped. I did small acts of kindness on a regular daily basis. At the time, I didn't know these acts would add up and help me become a more honorable person. Yet one day I woke up and realized that I had become respectable. Instead of being on the outside of the human community, I was back in it. I was home.

I was no longer a beast. I was more human than predator. I was again part of the human family. One of the most beautiful things that came from this is that I could now let in the love that others had for me.

To recover from a spiritual illness—addiction—I needed the help of spiritual principles or principles of betterment. Spirituality in its simplest form is the ability to connect with the healing properties of spiritual principles and allow them to direct our lives. In this way, we become "principled." Our spirit is renewed.

Remember Ted in the opening scene of part 1? He hesitated, then decided to put aside his frustrations of the day and help his wife, Maggie, with her frustrations over the broken lamp. In doing so, he placed a spiritual principle of support ahead of his own desire to whine or complain. This is how love is created and sustained. As Maggie hears Ted reminding her not to argue about being late, she is placing the spiritual principle of restraint ahead of her own anger and frustration. Again, love is sustained. Even young David, sitting in "The Chair," is able to consider how his mother might feel about her favorite lamp lying in pieces. Empathy is an essential principle of love.

Family is where we're first taught or *not taught* to place spiritual principles before our narrower egos.

## Principles in Action

As humans, we are spiritually responsible for bringing principles of betterment to life through our actions; we are responsible for becoming their representatives. For example, when we repeatedly act out of respect, we become respectable and eventually respected. Others experience dignity when we treat them respectfully. As we become "principles in action," we contribute the spirit of these principles to the world, and in exchange we feel the peace and serenity that they hold. Serenity is a by-product of living by and staying attached to principles of betterment.

But this means that we must put these principles into *action*. Principles are just concepts until we make them a part of our everyday lives. We can speak all we want about love, but we're not loving until our actions embody this principle. When our actions resemble love, most often we need not speak of love—our actions speak for themselves. Twelve Step programs differentiate between those who "walk the walk" and those who "talk the talk." A big difference exists between living a principled life and merely talking about it.

All of this may sound well and good, but it doesn't seem very practical, or it would be too time-consuming, or we have enough to deal with right now. . . . Such resistance to change demonstrates a deeper resistance to living a life directed by principles. It is natural to resist change to some degree. Change always involves fear, loss, and grief. However, when we live by principles, we become less resistant, more open to change. The more we surrender our egos over to principles, the more accustomed we'll get to it, and the less scary it will become to be vulnerable in our relationships.

Conversely, if we defend our egos against higher principles, we become more afraid and less open to a spiritual transformation. We decide it's best to go it alone, to do it our way; we're less willing to be vulnerable and change.

At times, all of us become so afraid of change that we resist it and stop our growth and development. When we do this, the pain (guilt) of being separate from our principles emerges. Our conscience may remind us of them and bring us back in line with who we are and who we want to become. The addict, however, uses the intoxication experience to avoid or deaden this pain and in so doing slows down or prohibits spiritual growth. For the addict, guilt often becomes a trigger to use.

To better understand how couples and families create love and meaning, and choose to live their lives according to spiritual principles, let us first work to understand the nature of being human.

# CHAPTER 2

# HUMAN DRIVES

As human beings, we make choices that determine what type of life we will lead. These choices, in turn, are determined by the *drives*, or impulses, that we live by. A drive is our collective desires, beliefs, personal histories, and attitudes that have become strong enough to direct a course of action. Four major human drives are ultimately responsible for how we choose to live. They are the drives for

- connection
- meaning
- pleasure
- power

How we weave these four drives together in our lives dictates much of our behavior. All are necessary; none are right; none are wrong; all are neutral. We need to develop skills that allow us to comfortably use and live within each of these drives. If we live out of only one or two of these drives, we'll be incomplete.

For example, a person who spends every waking minute of the day working to acquire more power does so at great expense to the other drives. A client of mine who had spent his adult life working to be powerful said: "I've achieved much and become very powerful and important within my company, but the cost has been great to me and my family. I have no meaningful relationships. I can't walk through the door of my own home and find anyone truly glad to see me. I can't remember the last time anyone simply smiled at me." This middle-aged man sought help because he had developed only those skills necessary to acquire power. He didn't know how to create pleasure or sustain meaning in his life. He had reached his goal only to find it empty and lacking what he most desired—his loved ones.

In one of his wonderful books, Carlos Castaneda talks of running into Don Juan, an old Indian sorcerer, in Mexico City. Don Juan is dressed in a beautiful three-piece suit, is carrying a gold-tipped walking cane, and is sitting on a park bench feeding the pigeons. When Castaneda asked him what he was doing and why he was dressed so finely, Don Juan replied, "Practicing. One must know how to live and fit into many different worlds." We all have many worlds. Pleasure, power, and meaning are three of them. We must learn to feel connected to them all.

## Internal Value of Drives

The order and value we assign to these drives is critical (see figure 1). Yet most of us never examine, let alone take responsibility for, how these drives are ordered inside of us. If we are to grow spiritually, we need to become responsible for their priority in our lives. How we order these drives determines our views, beliefs, behaviors, and principles—or lack of them.

# The Pleasure, Power, Connection, and Meaning Framework

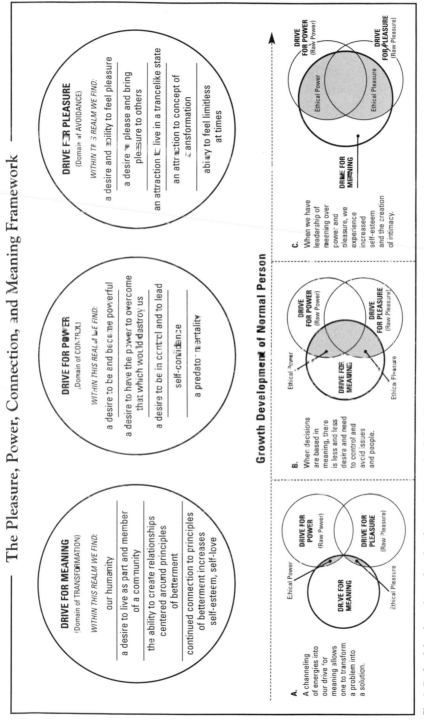

**DRIVE FOR MEANING**
(Domain of TRANSFORMATION)

*WITHIN THIS REALM WE FIND:*

our humanity

a desire to live as part and member of a community

the ability to create relationships centered around principles of betterment

continued connection to principles of betterment increases self-esteem, self-love

**DRIVE FOR POWER**
(Domain of CONTROL)

*WITHIN THIS REALM WE FIND:*

a desire to be and become powerful

a desire to have the power to overcome that which would destroy us

a desire to be in control and to lead

self-confidence

a predator mentality

**DRIVE FOR PLEASURE**
(Domain of AVOIDANCE)

*WITHIN THIS REALM WE FIND:*

a desire and ability to feel pleasure

a desire to please and bring pleasure to others

an attraction to live in a trancelike state

an attraction to concept of transformation

ability to feel limitless at times

## Growth Development of Normal Person

**A.** A channeling of energies into our drive for meaning allows one to transform a problem into a solution.

DRIVE FOR POWER (Raw Power)
DRIVE FOR PLEASURE (Raw Pleasure)
DRIVE FOR MEANING
Ethical Power
Ethical Pleasure

**B.** When decisions are based in meaning, there is less and less desire and need to control and avoid issues and people.

DRIVE FOR POWER (Raw Power)
DRIVE FOR PLEASURE (Raw Pleasure)
DRIVE FOR MEANING
Ethical Power
Ethical Pleasure

**C.** When we have leadership of meaning over power and pleasure, we experience increased self-esteem and the creation of intimacy.

DRIVE FOR POWER (Raw Power)
DRIVE FOR PLEASURE (Raw Pleasure)
DRIVE FOR MEANING
Ethical Power
Ethical Pleasure

**Fig. 1:** Each of the three drives found within us desires to lead. Our drive for meaning needs to be what we turn to in solving the issues that life gives us. When the spiritual principles found within this drive are combined with the energies of the other drives and put into action, growth occurs and self-esteem is created. The spiritual principles embedded within our drive for meaning hold the ability to heal wounds and to transform problems into solutions.

The four human drives on page 17 are listed in descending order of importance. The drive for connection is most critical because it's present in each of the other drives. It propels us to seek out spiritual principles, loving relationships, and answers to the paradoxes we face in life. In its most developed form, the drive for connection is our desire for unity with all that is spiritual, causing us to seek perfect love. It is the spiritual craving for the unattainable inside of us. The drive for connection, however, will be limited by our personal development.

We all tend to connect only with those who share our beliefs. Often, we look for support from those who agree with us and can reflect back to us our own worldview. In relationships with such people, we find comfort and feel less alone. However, this egocentric approach limits us. We may become afraid to reach for higher levels of meaning and new ways to view the world. Our natural resistance to change opposes our drive for connection and causes us to seek an "easier, softer way" to get through life. Without meaningful connections and purpose that evolves from them, we become individuals reduced only to seeking comfort and safety.

## The Drive for Meaning

If we focus primarily on power or pleasure, we end up incomplete beings. The pursuit of pleasure and power can't create meaning in an individual's life. It's a crippling illusion to believe otherwise.

Why, then, do so many people dedicate their lives to pleasure and power? The reasons are many. Many people are afraid of the sacrifice, discipline, and work needed to create meaningful lives, so they surround themselves with objects and symbols of pleasure and power for comfort. Some whose

lives are filled with emotional or physical pain pursue pleasure for relief. Others are taught as children that power and
pleasure are all-important. They watch their parents work
and sacrifice in the name of achieving power and the freedom to pursue pleasure. We all hear the constant cultural
chatter encouraging us to be first in everything we do. As a
society, deluged with images of fame and fortune, we are
misled to believe that if we are "number one," we will have
power—and with power comes meaning and pleasure.

Those who chase only pleasure and power eventually
feel empty because the spiritual craving for connection
to spiritual principles and meaning goes unfulfilled. In
addiction, spiritual cravings get reinterpreted as a desire for
pleasure and/or more power.* Addiction is a spiritual illness
in that it doesn't allow a person's drive for meaning to
become his primary operating drive. The objects and events
addicts or alcoholics attach to actually have no spirits.
They only mirror life or imitate it. Addicts have deluded
themselves into believing that they have found meaning in
their intoxication experience. What the addicts are actually pursuing is meaningless. Subsequently, they never find
the joy that love creates. This sentiment is echoed in the
meditation for November 4 in *Twenty-Four Hours a Day*, a
popular meditation book in recovery circles: "We cannot
find true happiness by looking for it. Seeking pleasure does
not bring happiness in the long run, only disillusionment.
Do not seek to have this fullness of joy by seeking pleasure.
It cannot be done that way. Happiness is a by-product of
living the right kind of a life."

---

* An old friend of mine, Chris Ringer, defined *addiction* as answering the
spiritual calling inside of us by going to the wrong address.

Meaning is not just an airy concept; it has a very practical purpose. When we create shared meaning with another, we become better at resolving and living with the complexities of life. Think of meaning as the blood of a family. It runs through veins and arteries unseen, little attention paid to it until there is a cut or a wound. Meaning within families will be rich or anemic depending on the spiritual principles that flow between family members. What makes meaning rich and deep-flowing are the principles of betterment and how they are acted out in each family. The principles heal the problems and wounds that exist in all families.

Remember the Jensens? Principles of betterment—patience, restraint, care, kindness, listening, and assistance—guided this family and saved the evening. Ted, Maggie, and even David knew on some deep, intuitive level that the future of the family lies in how well they deal with each crisis.

In all families there will be exchanges that aren't worth the trade. You sacrifice for the family only to be told how much more the others have sacrificed. You practice restraint only to see others out of control. Thus, families work on percentages.

When our drives for power and pleasure preserve the instinctual sides of our beings, the drive for meaning preserves the spiritual side of our beings. Each has a voice; each wants to be heard. Together they form a "committee." We can feel and listen as they debate about the best way to handle our dilemmas. We often struggle to maintain a working relationship among our drives. Who we are as individuals inevitably is determined by the relationship we have with these three drives and which one is given the leadership role.

## Why Meaning Must Be Most Important

Meaning helps us resolve and live with the complex nature of life. Life is full of contradictions that require resolutions. We are asked to feel *and* to reason. At times, we feel both blessed *and* cursed. We are conscious of our ability to create *and* to destroy. We see endless possibilities *and* at the same time sense our limitations. We intuit two sides to every coin but view only one. By solving life's paradoxes, we acquire new perspectives, skills, and information. We learn how to bring things together instead of tearing them apart. We learn to join and not separate.

Each one of us yearns and seeks to embrace life. We believe in relationships and are attracted to mysteries and meaning. We also are attracted to destructive aspects of the world. Sometimes, we want to see how close to the edge we can get without falling over into the abyss. We may not trust relationships and are attracted to raw power and pleasure.

Again neither of these aspects of our personality are good or bad, right or wrong. Growing up, most of us learn to be ashamed and to pretend we don't have a dark or instinctual side. However, without both, we wouldn't need to make spiritual choices.

The interplay between the creative and destructive sides of our personality can cause anxiety, pain, and resistance to change. We may wish we could remove this interplay from our consciousness. The most common form of numbing is denial. We pretend we are not part of the species that is responsible for Three Mile Island, apartheid, Auschwitz, Hiroshima, the killing fields of Cambodia, and the slaughter in Rwanda. We deny that we are part animal. Ernest Becker in his book *Escape from Evil* argues that most evil in this world results from people pretending that they are not animals. Ironically this denial increases the destructive nature of our beings. We become less, not more, able to control our actions. This is the very denial that the addictive process feeds on.

Addiction can be viewed as an illness that suppresses the life instinct. It prevents individuals from forming and sustaining meaningful connections with family, friends, themselves, their Higher Power, and community. Denial numbs our humanity and community spirit, letting our instinct become dominant. We close down to life and turn to our dark side.

Love requires an openness and willingness to see all sides—dark and light—of the world. Love bonds these two aspects of our personality into one spiritual force. A faith in love is a belief that love can truly transform death into life, animal into human. A recovering addict I know who is dying of AIDS said: "I think it's only because of my AIDS that I can now get sober. Before this, I would never have taken life seriously enough to get into recovery. I want to die a human being, not as an addict."

## When the Drive for Pleasure Ranks First

If we seek pleasure above all else, we paradoxically destroy our ability to create and experience authentic pleasure. Existentialist and Holocaust survivor Viktor Frankl stated it well in *Man's Search for Meaning*: "Pleasure is and must remain a side-effect or by-product and is destroyed and spoiled to the degree to which it is made a goal in itself." The addict doesn't realize that by chasing after pleasure she eventually becomes incapable of experiencing pleasure.

Authentic, or principled, pleasure is a by-product of using the principles of betterment. Authentic pleasure is also *ethical pleasure*—it seeks not to hurt others or self.

We seek out beautiful sunsets, experience joy in helping others, or spend an evening listening to our favorite music. Authentic pleasure has lasting quality and can bring comfort long after the event is over.

Raw, or nonprincipled, pleasure, on the other hand, stems from the direct stimulation of one's senses. It knows no ethics. Raw pleasure fades quickly after stimulation of the senses subsides and holds little if any long-lasting meaning or benefits. It can be injected, imbibed, or swallowed. Authentic pleasure requires effort, whereas raw pleasure requires only stimulation of certain pleasure centers of the brain. Authentic pleasure seems to involve the entire mind and heart, which then stimulate pleasure centers. Conversely, raw pleasure seems to start from direct stimulation of the pleasure centers and then spreads to our thinking.

Formula for authentic pleasure:

quality of experience + values + thinking = pleasure

Formula for raw pleasure:

stimulation of pleasure centers = thinking + type of experience

Though more lasting, authentic pleasure, which involves our thinking, is often less intense and trancelike than raw pleasure. Raw pleasure, because it primarily involves the pleasure centers of the brain (preverbal, prethought regions of our minds), is primarily a trance. This is what makes raw pleasure so attractive to some people. Think of the addictive gambler sitting hour after hour in front of a slot machine. Random, nonsequential thoughts go through this person's mind, but none are as important as the images before his eyes. Though aware of his surroundings, he is in a trance. If someone interrupts him, he becomes irritated and upset. He wants no real social connection, because he already feels free and at peace as long as his electric morphine continues. This addictive trance eventually breaks down parts of life that require logic. The addict works to become detached from the responsibility created by the principles of betterment. Guilt and conscience shut down.[*]

As the pleasure-oriented person steps outside of everyday life and its realities, she becomes unskilled in the elements needed to have a truly meaningful and pleasurable life. She is like the person who has a balloon payment on a house due and has not put anything aside to pay for it. She will lose everything.

The pleasure-oriented person believes the purpose of life is to experience pleasure. Such people become seekers of two things: First, they seek the trancelike state that raw pleasure brings, and second, they seek to avoid life's anxiety and pain. Struggling is seen as meaningless unless it brings more pleasure. In fact, struggling is seen as failure, because it means the person cannot produce pleasure. Thus, avoidance becomes this person's primary strategy for dealing with life.

When the drive for pleasure is most dominant in a person, he will experience a destructive intensity, grief, self-centeredness, and a distortion of time and reason.

---

[*] Because the person is attaching to the preverbal, prethought regions of his brain, he is also attaching to the presocial aspect of his personality. Guilt and conscience require thinking; not thinking equals no guilt, no conscience. Guilt and conscience are generated from our social relationship and how well we honor the principles needed to get along as humans. Thus, the trancelike state the addict goes into has little if any conscience attached to it. Guilt becomes merely a faint voice, if a voice at all, until the trance experience is over. Then it often becomes so loud that it changes form and becomes shame.

## Intensity

Pleasure-oriented people determine the value for any individual or object by the pleasure that person or object can produce. If a person or an object becomes incapable of providing pleasure, it becomes worthless and is often discarded. For this reason, a highly pleasurable drug is often more important than a good relationship. A drug is far more capable of providing continuous pleasure than another person. In a perverse way, drugs are more dependable than people.

Individuals operating from this orientation mistakenly define love by intensity. The addict mistakes a sensory experience for a spiritual experience. Love gets judged by whether it produces good or bad feelings. Good feelings are more important than truth. Love then gets reduced to a "feel-good experience." The pleasure-oriented person regularly falls "in and out" of love. When intensity fades, love fades. Such people often describe themselves as "love crazed" or as having been bitten by the "love bug." Because they have little influence, control, and responsibility over the sensations they feel and define as love, they often end up "victims of love."

The myth here is that love should feel good. In truth, love doesn't always feel good. Love is not primarily a sensory experience. When we focus only on the feel-good aspects of love, we monitor sensations and emotions instead of behaviors, principles, and attitudes.

Because pleasure-oriented people are tied to the impulsiveness of sensations, their relationships are often unstable. They often declare their love dead when good feelings fade. They believe that the more intense the feelings, the more love there must be. For example, abusive families often define the intensity inherent in violence as "proof" of love. "He only hits me because he loves me," a victim may say. "I did it because I love you, and it was the only way I could get through to you," the perpetrator argues. "I did it for your own good." Violence, though intense, is never part of love. As Mahatma Gandhi said, "I object to violence because when it appears to do good, the good is only temporary; the evil it does is permanent."

## Grief

Pleasure is a temporary state. It fades over time. Emotions are not constant. Pleasure-oriented people unknowingly attach themselves to a process that contains within it another—the grieving process. Because the addict's pleasure or sensations are always ending, she lives in perpetual grief. This grief may evolve into long-term depression.

Though objects or events that create pleasure are reliable and predictable, the pleasure *always* fades. Therefore, a person who judges himself by his ability to create and sustain pleasure is doomed never to feel successful or competent in any *continuous* manner.

## Self-centeredness

Because raw pleasure is a sensory, internal experience, it's a very private experience. Selfishness and self-centeredness are pleasure's main by-products. Addicts don't stop to think about what is best for them or others while they are intoxicated. They just do what feels good now.

*Alcoholics Anonymous* explains, "Selfishness—self-centeredness! That, we think, is the root of our troubles." The authors of these words knew that raw pleasure is based on personal preference. The addict who chases after pleasure is pulled into himself; he unknowingly becomes as self-absorbed as the cat chasing its own tail.

## *Distortion of Time and Reason*

In terms of time, each moment becomes all-important as the addict strives to squeeze as much pleasure out of it as possible. The addict seeks to control, heighten, and enhance the intensity of raw pleasure. During these moments, one's values, principles, and integrity are sacrificed. Meaning and love are also sacrificed. The pleasure-oriented individual will sacrifice the future for moments of immediate pleasure. Everything is sacrificed for an intense experience of now. Why delay any pleasure for tomorrow? Why let the past sour today's pleasure? The addict lives only in the present.

Reason has little to do with raw pleasure. Rational parts of the brain aren't needed to produce raw pleasure; only the more primitive lower regions are necessary to monitor one's senses. Reason and its skills atrophy over time when they are not used. An addict can easily fall into more primitive, emotionally reactive states.

A life dedicated to pleasure produces no real power or meaning. The intoxication experience produces only the illusion of power and meaning. As the trance fades, so does the sense of power and meaning. Meaning and a sense of personal empowerment never become fully internalized. As a result, fear becomes a predominant underlying condition for the pleasure-seeking person. He senses that he is not developing any of the internal strengths or skills needed to feel empowered.

# Summary of the
# Pleasure-Oriented Personality

| | |
|---|---|
| **VISION:** | Life is painful, but the pleasure you can get out of it is what makes life worth living. |
| **GOAL:** | To avoid the pain and anxiety produced by the paradoxes one faces in life. |
| **SENSE OF TIME:** | Main focus is on the moment and on getting as much pleasure or avoiding as much pain as possible right now. |
| **VALUE:** | Is defined by an event's ability, an object's ability, or a person's ability to produce pleasurable feelings. Objects often become more important than people because they are more reliable and predictable in their ability to produce pleasurable feelings. |
| **BY-PRODUCT:** | Grief is the primary by-product for the person whose primary drive is pleasure. Feelings always fade, thus the person is attached to a grief process. Over time the person can become severely depressed. Other effects cause a destructive intensity, self-centeredness, and a distortion of time and reason. |

Fig. 2

# Characteristics of a
# Pleasure-Oriented Life

- Emotions are always temporary states; thus, life is unstable.

- Person sets up a reactive lifestyle.

- Relationships are only as important as the pleasure they can provide.

- Ego inflates to unhealthy proportions.

- Intensity is more important than intimacy.

- No real power develops inside the person. Sense of power comes from intoxication experience. As trance fades so does sense of power; thus, power is never internalized.

- Person increasingly operates from instinctive animal side of being.

- Person develops a scanning perspective: scanning the environment for that which will bring pleasure. Thus, he or she develops an external locus of control, not internal.

**Fig. 3**

## Nancy's Story

*I just wanted to feel great all the time, and I didn't care how it happened. When I used cocaine, it was as if heaven had chosen to come live inside of me. I loved the sensations it created and the way I felt when I used. Just the thought of getting high brought great pleasure to me. It wasn't long after I started using that I was getting high as often as I could.*

*Cocaine, I believed, could help me discover all the different ways there were to achieve and receive pleasure. It also seemed to open up that part of my mind that controlled my sexual thoughts and desires. I found myself thinking a lot about sex and having different sexual partners. I started going to parties where drugs and sex were the central themes. I was in heaven—no, I was heaven. All it seemed to cost was the price of getting high. The people around me, mainly my family, didn't understand what I had discovered. I told myself they were afraid little people who weren't willing to take the risks needed to embrace pleasure at its fullest. Sex and drugs were my gateways to a new world.*

*I thought it would never get old, but it did. Cocaine aged me in the process. Pleasure was the web, and I was caught. When I finally looked around, it was as if life had gone ahead without me. My old friends had families and were making something out of their lives. But me? I was alone except for my drugs and my sex partners. What I had were memories, and many of those were not the type I really wanted to share. What had a life of pleasure given me? A fear of the future and poor health. I felt so far behind that I would get high just to forget who and where I was. It got to the point that I*

*hated to think. I wasn't able to sort out what had
happened. Why had this beautiful plan of pleasure,
pleasure, pleasure gone wrong? My mind was tired and
so was I. That was the real reason I went to treatment.
(Nancy is sober today and rebuilding her life, but is
HIV positive.)*

## When the Drive for Power Ranks First

Power, like pleasure, is not inherently good or bad, but it
needs to be contained and led by higher principles to be
transformed into ethical power. If this doesn't happen, it
degenerates into darker forms. In his book *Power and
Innocence: A Search for the Sources of Violence*, Rollo May
describes five types of power. In order of importance, they
are: (1) integrative; (2) nutrient; (3) competitive; (4) manipulative; and (5) exploitative. May explains that the lower
the form of power (exploitative being the lowest), the more
void it is of higher principles. The lower, rawer forms
of power are antirelationship and antilove. The more
evolved forms of power are prorelationship, prolove, and
proprinciples.

People who seek power for power's sake acquire it at the
expense of meaning. For them, power is security. Such
people operate primarily from May's three lowest types of
power: exploitative, manipulative, and competitive. Their
goal is to acquire and accumulate power for power's sake.
Meaning is seen as useful, but secondary to power. They see
the person in power as the one who defines what is or what

is not meaningful. This reasoning allows the individual seeking power to justify and distance himself from his own exploitative and manipulative behavior.

When the drive for power ranks first, life's struggles are mainly about acquiring more power. The person struggles first to create a power base, then to keep it. He struggles to get power away from others, as they struggle to get power away from him. Life becomes a vicious struggle for control.

The power seeker attempts to control each moment to achieve his sense of power, status, and self-confidence. In terms of how this person views time, moments are important, if he can control them. Control becomes critical.

For the power-centered person, self-confidence is seen as self-esteem. In reality, however, they are entirely different. We feel self-confident when we're comfortable with the power and control we have in a given situation. Self-esteem, on the other hand, is an internal strength we gain by living according to the principles of betterment. It is enduring and doesn't change from situation to situation. Normally there is a relationship between self-confidence and self-esteem, with each helping to raise or lower the other. In addiction, however, behaviors that increase one's sense of power and self-confidence are usually acts of self-betrayal, which inevitably lower one's self-esteem. Thus, in addiction the relationship between self-confidence and self-esteem is inverse. For that reason, we often find addicts with high self-confidence and low self-esteem. The addict may appear self-assured and confident, but inside is full of doubt and fear.

By controlling the moment, one receives temporary relief from the fears and doubts that a power-focused lifestyle creates. Self-confidence increases. However, power, like pleasure, fades; as it does, fears and doubts return. The person then seeks other situations or people to control and dominate in order to drown out uncertainty and reestablish a sense of well-being.

## Power Struggles

Power-centered people are constantly involved in some type of power struggle.* They believe that life's struggles get solved by deciding what is "right" and summoning all the power at their disposal for the rightness of their cause. They fail to see their rightness as an extension of their own inflated ego, as the loss of a healthy self-questioning, and they often become self-righteous as they gather more and more power. They don't understand that being right and finding the truth are most often two different things.

Struggles are seen as failures unless they produce a win in your column and an increased power base. Pleasure also comes from acquiring power and then using it to dominate others. The bully truly enjoys the fear expressed by her victims. The screamer loves the sound of his own voice; all he hears is the power embedded in his vocal intimidation.

Couples that become power-centered allow only one person to be right at any given time. They set up a "king or queen of the mountain" mentality. Individuals learn to defend only their own rightness, instead of learning how to

---

* The power-centered person is involved in power struggles, whereas the meaning-centered person is involved in integrity struggles. Thus, the power-centered person is struggling to get close to that which she sees as the source of power, whereas the meaning-centered person is struggling to figure out and find the truth and get as close to it as possible. If one is successful in power struggles, more power is acquired and ego is inflated. If one is successful in integrity struggles, one acquires more dignity, more understanding of the principles one was struggling with, and deflation of ego.

embrace and defend the correctness of their partner's views. They ignore any truths that may be in front of them and keep fighting until someone submits. Being right is experienced as power and being wrong as weakness. The "righter" you are, the more power you hold, and the more power you hold, the more righteous you feel. Might makes right. The winner in these battles gets to define how the problem will be viewed. This definition often bears little resemblance to the true nature of the problem. What is meaningful is subordinate and determined by what is powerful. This primary dynamic takes place in the addictive family.

Addictive families are systems dominated by and structured around power. The illness of addiction (like all other major illnesses) controls all members. When the chief carrier of the addiction—the addict—is present, the *true* family shuts down. For protection, the family goes into emotional hiding and stops being a family.

People who seek to control wrongly believe that their power changes others. However, power doesn't change people; only meaning (acquiring or losing it) can do this. Power can conquer but it cannot convert. Power can get others to *act* totally different while no true change has occurred. The illness of addiction is the perfect example of this.

The power-oriented person also believes power equals value. An individual's value is determined by the amount of power he is seen as having. If someone is viewed as not having power, then such a person is considered ineffectual and has little if any value. People and relationships that can't increase one's power base are not important.

### Dominant and Submissive Relationships

The power-centered person most often experiences love as being over or under someone. Love gets defined as being lovingly dominant or submissive to another, which is in truth dependency. The dominant partner is as dependent as the submissive partner. However, for the dominant person, having another submit to her ego creates a false sense of power. This inflated sense of power is then defined as love. Submission is considered as proof of one's love by both the dominant and the submissive members.*

This form of "love" is very unstable because acts of independence are attacked as nonloving, and they create relationship crises. Interactions are not judged by quality but by the dominance and/or submission content. The clearer and more accepted the dominant and/or submissive roles are, the more calm and stable the system or relationship seems to be. In the addictive family, all members are pressured to submit to the addictive process.

Families, individuals, and couples that operate from this framework are constantly engaged in power struggles about who is right and who is wrong. Such power struggles involve situations where one person must either go along (and in so doing lose his dignity) or fight the other for dominance. Right and wrong become all-important, though the battles rarely have anything to do with the truth. Being right for some people brings a sense of privilege and the illusion of security. The "right one" secretly or not-so-secretly

---

* Sometimes people who are dominant in their public lives are submissive in their private lives. This role reversal is seen as and felt as surrendering to love in a deep and meaningful way, when in reality it is just a reversal of roles. On its most basic level there is no difference between the dominant and submissive personalities; both see and get a sense of increased power from their position and role.

believes she is smarter and better than others, but in reality the right one is just the dominant one. In addictive families, the addict often comes across as self-righteous because of the power she holds.

### Fear and Blaming

Blame is a major by-product in a family that has power as its central organizing principle. Blame is a defense mechanism used to save and protect one's power base. To admit being wrong feels like giving up power. It shakes the person's self-confidence. Because of this, members of addictive families are not taught that surrendering one's ego is an important skill of love. Instead, they are taught to feel ashamed if they surrender. They learn to cover up their mistakes or blame others for them instead of seeing shortcomings as opportunities for growth.

A life centered around power is a scary life primarily for two reasons. First, you are always uncertain whether your power can still get others to submit. Subsequently, you must always be testing, arguing, and requiring others to accept your point of view or policy. Second, you always know there are others who want to acquire your power to increase their own. You feel like the gunfighter waiting for the next person to step in the saloon to earn a reputation at your expense. Power breeds fear, and the antidote for this fear is thought to be more power.

### Objects of Power

For the power-centered person, objects that symbolize power are as important as people. This type of person always needs the most up-to-date things: the newest computer, the finest wines, the best gold watches, the most expensive car, or the biggest antique gun collection.

# Summary of the
# Power-Oriented Personality

| | |
|---|---|
| **VISION:** | Life is a struggle to get as much power as possible, and this is what will bring you true comfort and pleasure. |
| **GOAL:** | To get as much power as you can and push for what you see and believe is "right." |
| **SENSE OF TIME:** | Main focus is on the moment, *but on controlling it.* You are to make the moment work for you. |
| **VALUE:** | Is defined by the potential for power an event, an object, or a person is seen as holding. Status symbols are important because of the power they represent. |
| **BY-PRODUCT:** | Blaming and fear are the primary by-products for the person whose primary drive is power. You are always aware that there are others who have more power and that power is yours only as long as you can hold on to it. Fear of getting older is often part of this person's personality. |

Fig. 4

Whatever the objects, they hold a special meaning for that person and make him feel superior to others. They are statements about how important he is. Expensive possessions produce pleasurable feelings. They're meant to scare off others by sending a message of power. Often individuals, couples, or families in this trap spend more than their budgets in an attempt to acquire status and power symbols.

Total dedication to this power orientation produces a hedonistic, self-centered, and paranoid lifestyle. As with pleasure, when power becomes more important than meaning, ego inflates.

## Characteristics of a Power-Oriented Life

- Right-wrong is all-important.

- Relationships become dominant-submissive.

- Blame becomes the primary defense mechanism and a way to keep power.

- Person sets up a reactive lifestyle.

- Power is seen as producing pleasure.

- Relationships are only as important as the power they can provide.

- Ego inflates to unhealthy proportions.

- Person increasingly operates from instinctive animal side of being.

- Person gains power from being either the victimizer or the victim, but the person always ends up as a predator of self and others.

**Fig. 5**

### Jake's Story

*I love power. Always have, always will. I want as much of it as I can get. I've never backed down to anyone or anything. To surrender and admit to being wrong is next to impossible for me. That's partially why my addiction almost killed me and may yet.*

*I love drinking. Those first few drinks make me feel invincible. I often get in verbal battles with people when drinking. A few times, I've ended up in fistfights. No one gets to tell me what to do or how to think. Once a man with a bat stopped me when I was drunk. I turned it on him and beat him up, put him in the hospital.*

*I have succeeded at everything I've put my mind to. That's mainly why I'm afraid to really try and get sober; it's the only thing I'm not sure I could do.*

*Life is good—my only problem is I always end up alone, except for alcohol. Even though I'm a good person, if I get into a power struggle, I'll do whatever is needed to win. I have tons of friends and acquaintances, mainly people who feel protected and safe around my power—you know, like the little fish who hang around the sharks. But anyone whom I've loved I've chased out of my life because I always have to be right, even when I'm dead wrong. I've been married a couple of times, but they both left me because of my temper and the way I get when I've been drinking. If someone tries to stand up to me, I just get louder, get more intense, and swear at them until they back down. People say I'm a wonderful guy unless I'm drinking; then I get crazy.*

*I've tried AA and had some periods of success, but I've never truly surrendered. I hate the term* powerlessness. *(Jake enjoys periods of short-term sobriety followed by*

*binge drinking and abusive behavior toward himself and others.)*

## How Do We Develop Our Drive for Meaning?

Human beings grow into meaning. As children, we seek pleasure. We play, and through play, we create new worlds and ideas. After a while, we discover that we can influence and at times control those around us. We discover power. We learn that power also can open up new worlds and ideas.

But something is missing. We want to be more than just entities that seek out pleasure and power. There's a craving, a longing, deep inside of us. We want something more solid and more lasting than sensations can provide. We want to be more than just animals surviving in comfort. We seek transformation. We want to find and explore our humanity. So we pursue meaning.

Children begin this quest by asking why this and why that. Their heads and hearts are filled with endless questions: What makes an airplane fly? Where do clouds come from? Where does smoke go? Why do people get married? Why do people get divorced? Why do you drink so much?

We humans have been given the gift of sensations *and* reason. At some time we become, as Erich Fromm said, "life being aware of itself."* It's at this time that we start to

---

* In *The Art of Loving*, Fromm discusses how, as we become aware that we are life, we also become aware of our own separateness and how this awareness becomes the driving force inside us that pushes us to go out and connect with others.

develop our drive for meaning. But how do we turn a craving for meaning *into* meaning and then a life of love?

We do this by becoming skillful in the art of extracting meaning and truths from our experiences. We develop skills in this art by first identifying various principles of betterment and then becoming willing to be transformed by those principles. When we become attached to principles of betterment and put them before our desires, we rise above our sensory instincts. Our impulsiveness is now guided by principles instead of impulsiveness being our guide.

There are many principles of betterment. One important principle of betterment we need to develop and become very skillful at concerns choice and responsibility. Choice and responsibility are wings of the same bird and must work together. They have the power to lift us above the impulses of the moment and allow us to achieve new perspectives and skills and access other principles. Some of these principles are discussed below. They include ethical power, responsibility, the three Ss, and discipline.

### Choice-Points

Spirituality rarely comes about in any big, dramatic way. It is not often that a single event, sacred moment, or "hot flash" such as Bill W.'s (the cofounder of Alcoholics Anonymous) instantaneously transforms our lives. Rather, our spirituality usually grows over time, one moment or insight after another. These small daily moments make up the true essence of any loving relationship. If we're not honest during the day about what seems insignificant, we're not likely to be honest when the chips are down. If we can follow principles of betterment during our everyday activities, we'll be more successful in creating love and sustaining meaning in our relationships and families.

Created love requires taking responsibility for one's choices. All situations hold within them what are called choice-points—moments when we must slow down events or situations so that we can see the small choices we have within them. Slowing down time is a skill that becomes easier with practice. *Whatever we do repeatedly, we will get better at.* Discovering our choice-points in any given situation involves slowing or breaking time down into manageable sections, like "One day at a time" or one moment at a time. Choice-points are moments where we choose to either embrace principles of betterment or act in an unprincipled manner. We are faced with choice-points daily. Acknowledging that we have the ability to make choices is an admission of power and influence. It also speaks of responsibility. During these choice-points, we fight our spiritual battles. The sum of these moments and choices determines what our values are and what meaning our lives will have.

Often we try to pretend—mainly to ourselves—that these moments mean little. We might imagine that someone else controls them. We might believe our boss or spouse is in control of a final decision. However, if we avoid being responsible for ourselves, then we are doomed to be tied to whatever or whomever we hold responsible for our actions.

The task of holding ourselves accountable is not always easy. From time to time, we may find ourselves avoiding responsibility and blaming others for our pain and problems. Blame is a defense to avoid pain, but it actually ties us more tightly to that which has hurt or scared us. Blame is often impulsive and reactive. However, blaming is also a behavior stemming from a bad choice we have made. Blaming others only creates that which we sought to avoid—fear, anger, and pain. Whether or not we are living in an addictive family system, we can face what frightens us. We needn't let blaming turn us away or create anger. We can choose and take responsibility.

Remember, we have choice-points in any situation, even if the only choice is determining the attitude we take toward our own suffering. We needn't feel trapped like a victim. We might be living with an addict spouse, but we can choose to behave honorably, not dishonorably.

Being responsible for our choices creates ethical power. Choice is power. It allows freedom. Power comes from seeing and claiming the thousands of options we have. Freedom comes from exercising these options. The more responsible we become, the more options we create, and the more power and freedom we gain.

### Taking Personal and Collective Responsibility

The principles of betterment can affect our lives only if we first accept personal responsibility for them, which means we must have our own relationship with these principles. We must choose how connected we will be with these principles. Taking personal responsibility also means that we must help, mainly by example, others in their struggles to get closer to these principles.

Collective responsibility means that as a social collective body we are responsible for developing and promoting principles of betterment. It is our duty to bring life to principles; we are to be their stewards. Just as plants and flowers grow wild on their own, these principles of betterment exist on their own. But once you bring one or more of these wild plants or flowers into your home or interior life, you are then responsible for their growth and development. They are now dependent on you for their existence in your community. Principles of betterment, or spiritual principles, have been given to us, and if we care for them and work to develop them, they blossom as beautifully as any flower would in a garden.

Again, the only way they can develop and bloom is by our taking responsibility for them through our actions and behavior. This is the essence of spirituality. Through our individual and collective relationships to these principles, we will make this world a living heaven or a living hell. If we choose to live in a respectful manner, we add respect to the world. If we choose to operate without respect, then we're working to rid the world of respect. Because of this, we must be willing to submit, surrender, and sacrifice for love and the principles that bring it to life.

### The Three Ss: Submission, Surrender, and Sacrifice

We must each consider what will lead us through life. We will be led either by our own ego, by another's ego, or by higher spiritual principles. We've been given the ability to see, understand, and achieve higher thought and order, but to achieve this takes skill. If we choose higher principles, we'll need the skills of submission, surrender, and sacrifice that make a bridge to this higher level of being. Without them, we're left at the level of our individual needs and impulses. It's through higher principles that we learn to say no to ourselves.

### Submission

When we submit ourselves, we surrender to another's authority. Spiritually, this skill of submission is vital and must come first in our spiritual growth and recovery. We need to accept that there are higher principles more important than any one of us. These principles must become our loving authority. If we see ourselves as the highest authority, we answer only to ourselves. We would then be submitting to a very low-level authority—our own ego. In this case, we're reducing the size of the world down to one. To enlarge the world, we need to step outside ourselves and get past our own egos to principles of betterment. When we allow higher, or spiritual, principles to be our ultimate authority, we participate in our own ego transformation. We step out of a one-dimensional ego into a multidimensional world of spirituality.

To form truly intimate interpersonal relationships, a couple must submit their individual egos to higher principles for constant correction. Each must be willing to experience the other and be changed by the other. If this doesn't occur, then each will fight to control the other. Couples that are constantly fighting about who's right and who's wrong are the perfect example of individuals working to hold on to their own egos.

### Surrender

When we surrender, we give up our power to higher principles, and in so doing we strengthen these principles. But surrendering is also what makes us stronger. The act of surrendering to principles of betterment builds an internal and enduring strength called self-esteem. As we discussed earlier, self-esteem is different from self-confidence. Self-confidence stems from the development of the skills of acquiring *raw* power and control. Most often self-confidence is situational. We feel confident in situations we can control. Self-esteem, however, is steadfast, whether we are in control or not.

If people never surrendered their individual power for these principles, they would remain only principles with no real power behind them. For example, family is a concept that includes principles about how individuals are to act or behave within that unit. When individual family members surrender to these principles, they give power to the concept of family. The more power they give it, the stronger the concept of family becomes. Family is a principle, a concept, an idea, or a dream that we give life to. It doesn't have a life of its own as sensations do. Family members create meaning for the family when they place the principle of family before their individual personalities. Doing so promotes family unity. But if someone, like the addict, is not willing to surrender her power over to these principles, the family is weakened. Over time, other individuals also refuse to submit and surrender to the principles of family. The family gets weaker and weaker, until it doesn't have any power to effect change in anyone.

### Sacrifice

Do we use our power for a collective good or do we keep our power for ourselves? Choosing the latter leads to selfishness. Sacrifice is the act of giving up something of importance for something that has more importance. Spiritual growth requires us to sacrifice our egos. Our egos are very important to us, but they are even more important to the collective good.

Sacrificing brings perspective. We need to put ourselves in our proper place. Only when we're able to understand the proper role of ego can we gain a true perspective on our worth. As individuals, we are important, but we must also value the group, family, community, and humankind.

In my practice, I often work with high-powered people who truly don't understand why their spouses and children are upset when they don't spend time with them. Their reply is almost always the same: "Why are you upset? I give you everything you need." They don't understand that their true importance is not primarily as a provider, but as a family member.

Perspective and order become clear when we sacrifice. That is why sacrifice always involves giving up something of personal value. When we make a spiritual sacrifice, we always give up our ego for higher principles, as ego is what we humans value most.

For a relationship to form around the *concept of love* instead of the *sensations of love*, sacrifice must be a central organizing principle. Sacrifice weeds our psychological garden of excess ego. But again, all parties in the relationship must be willing to sacrifice. If this doesn't happen, an imbalance develops within the relationship that eats away at its core. The basic assumption behind all relationships is an agreement that life is better when it is shared with others. Under this agreement, each is to sacrifice for the privilege of being with another. If for any reason, such as addiction, someone goes back on this agreement, the relationship crumbles. In addiction, the addict unconsciously (because of denial) decides to go it alone. The family, especially the person's partner, feels the change in the agreement and reacts against it. The family senses the person is no longer willing to sacrifice for the good of the relationship. This endangers the relationship.

We all naturally resist sacrificing. It's difficult to imagine that values, such as submission, surrender, and sacrifice, are empowering. Some people even consider these values as disabling. As we step out of our egos and into these principles, we feel a sense of vulnerability. This vulnerability is often misinterpreted as weakness. However, Kahlil Gibran reminds us, "Tenderness and kindness are not signs of weakness and despair, but manifestations of strength and resolution."

## Discipline

Discipline is the ability to stay consistently attached to spiritual principles. Discipline takes the energy found in our impulsiveness and tempers it into determination. As Stephen Covey writes in *The 7 Habits of Highly Effective People,* "Self-mastery and self-discipline are the foundation of good relationships with others." I would add they're also the foundations of a good relationship with one's self.

Discipline can't be achieved by forcing yourself to *act* disciplined, at least not for very long. You must choose to *embrace* discipline. Forced discipline is just another name for punishment. In *The Art of Loving,* Erich Fromm writes: "Discipline should not be practiced like a rule imposed on oneself from the outside, but that it becomes an expression of one's own will; that it is felt as pleasant and that one slowly accustoms oneself to a kind of behavior which one would eventually miss, if one stopped practicing it." Discipline needn't be painful. Doing what is best for ourselves more often than not feels good and is agreeable to us.

There are two forms of discipline: *restrictive discipline* and *loving discipline*. Restrictive discipline is the lesser form of discipline. It feels like punishment and may create resentment and feelings of deprivation or restriction. On the other hand, loving discipline willingly sacrifices some of our choices. *No* is often the most loving word we can say to ourselves. We are defined as much by what we say *no* to as by what we say *yes* to. Selfishness has at its core the refusal to say no to oneself.

The Twelve Steps heavily emphasize discipline without ever mentioning it. Loving discipline is important in recovery. Discipline allows individuals to separate from the inflated ego that the addictive process creates. In

*Alcoholics Anonymous*, we read: "The alcoholic is an extreme example of self-will run riot, though he usually doesn't think so. Above everything, we alcoholics must be rid of this selfishness." Discipline helps us control the impulsive reactiveness that is an instinctive part of our beings. Discipline slows life down to a manageable pace. It is this very fact that makes discipline an ultra-important concept to addicts and their families in recovery. "One day at a time," when practiced, teaches discipline well.

Over time, discipline builds a *willing dependence* on principles. The longer we practice these principles, the deeper they work their way into the fiber of our beings. Thus, if we are consistent in our spiritual discipline, these principles become part of who we are. We *become* persons of integrity. We do not just understand care; we *become* caring. This is the "conscious contact" referred to in Step Eleven of Alcoholics Anonymous.* The person who operates in a disciplined manner creates an internal conscience, instead of an external conscience.

To practice spiritual discipline is to believe in the future. By living according to my principles today, I am taking charge of my future. When I work to hold back controlling comments to my wife, it's not just so the moment will go smoother. I am actually increasing my chances of acting in loving ways in the future.

---

* The Eleventh Step of Alcoholics Anonymous reads: "Sought through prayer and meditation to improve our conscious contact with God *as we understood Him*, praying only for knowledge of His will for us and the power to carry that out." Prayer and meditation are two behaviors that AA recommends its members become disciplined in. The clear purpose of this is an improved conscious contact with God, God being perfection of the principles of betterment.

Next, we'll examine how addiction can isolate an individual from his family and others and destroy his capacity to love (see figure 6). We will learn how addiction as an illness hampers an individual's ability to create and sustain intimate, meaningful, and loving relationships.

# The Pleasure, Power, Connection, and Meaning Framework

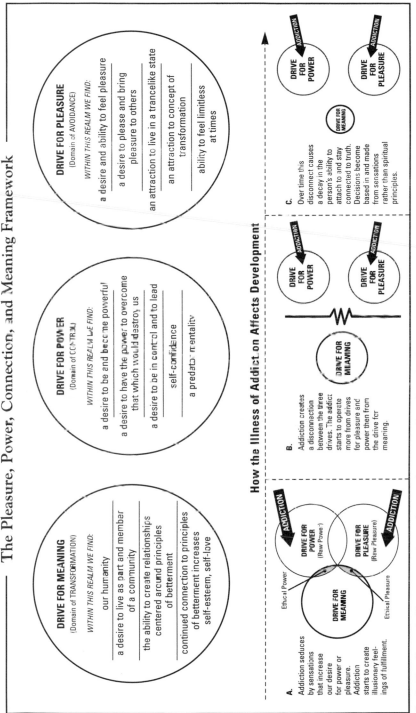

**DRIVE FOR MEANING**
(Domain of TRANSFORMATION)

*WITHIN THIS REALM WE FIND:*

our humanity

a desire to live as part and member of a community

the ability to create relationships centered around principles of betterment

continued connection to principles of betterment increases

self-esteem, self-love

**DRIVE FOR POWER**
(Domain of CONTROL)

*WITHIN THIS REALM WE FIND:*

a desire to be and become powerful

a desire to have the power to overcome that which would destroy us

a desire to be in control and to lead

self-confidence

a predatory mentality

**DRIVE FOR PLEASURE**
(Domain of AVOIDANCE)

*WITHIN THIS REALM WE FIND:*

a desire and ability to feel pleasure

a desire to please and bring pleasure to others

an attraction to live in a trancelike state

an attraction to concept of transformation

ability to feel limitless at times

## How the Illness of Addict on Affects Development

**A.** Addiction seduces by sensations that increase our desire for power or pleasure. Addiction starts to create illusionary feel-ings of fulfillment.

Ethical Power

**DRIVE FOR POWER** (Raw Power)

**DRIVE FOR PLEASURE** (Raw Pleasure)

**DRIVE FOR MEANING**

Ethical Pleasure

ADDICTION

ADDICTION

**B.** Addiction creates a disconnection between the three drives. The addict starts to operate more from drives for pleasure and power then from the drive for meaning.

DRIVE FOR POWER — ADDICTION

DRIVE FOR PLEASURE — ADDICTION

DRIVE FOR MEANING

**C.** Over time this disconnect causes a decay in the person's ability to attach to and stay connected to truth. Decisions become based in and made from sensations rather than spiritual principles.

DRIVE FOR POWER — ADDICTION

DRIVE FOR PLEASURE — ADDICTION

DRIVE FOR MEANING

**Fig. 6:** The illness of addiction enters by a seduction of sensations. By making the "high" more important than relationships and spiritual principles, a disconnect between the three drives is created. A person's decisions are now based on what best stimulates sensations rather than on spiritual principles; on what feels good rather than what is good. This disconnect doesn't allow the energies of the drives for power and pleasure to be channeled into the drive for meaning; thus the drive for meaning becomes subordinate to the drives for power and pleasure.

# STAGES OF FAMILY ADDICTION

# Introduction to Part 2

## Scene 2

In dread, Ted stands outside the front door of his home. His son, David, had called earlier. "She's at it again," David said. Ted takes a deep breath and opens the door. David, now sixteen, is in the kitchen, standing at the stove stirring beans and franks in a pot. He looks up and glances at his father. "She's in the bedroom."

"How bad?" Ted asks.

"She's been worse, but it's not pretty." Communication these days consists of short, quick statements.

Ted walks toward the bedroom. Not anxious to see his wife, he stops at the table where mail lies and opens a bill from a local department store. The bill only reminds him of the phone call from the collection agency. He
discovered then the existence of another charge account. Soon he'll have to call his parents again and ask for money, which means he'll have to listen to their suggestions and theories about what ails Maggie.

Ted has tried everything. He has hidden her bottles, stopped at the liquor store and asked them to not sell to his wife, took her to therapists, threatened divorce, poured water into her whiskey bottles, and extracted promises from her that she'd never drink again. He would yell at her; she'd cry. He'd cry, and she'd yell at him. Nothing worked.

When Ted reaches the bedroom and tries to open the door, he can't. Maggie has pushed the dresser against it. Ted leans into it with all his might. He feels angry, then fearful when the door opens wide enough for him to squeeze into the room. He sees his wife half off the bed and her head inches above the floor. Blood is smeared on her cheek. When Ted stoops and sees that the wound is minor, his fear turns to despair and disgust.

"Supper's ready," says David, who suddenly appears at the door.

"Did you know she was bleeding?"

"Yeah, but it didn't look bad and I had to get supper on. I'm going out soon," David replies with indifference.

"She could have bled to death!" Ted shouts.

"No. She couldn't have. I've seen worse." David is right. Twice before she needed stitches from a fall.

Ted pushes the dresser back against the wall. After he and David move Maggie to the center of the bed, they leave the room, close the door behind them, and return to the kitchen. For fifteen minutes, they eat in silence. When finished, David stands up and heads toward the door. "I'll be home later."

Ted wants to hug him, tell him life at home will get better, but his shame and despair keep him silent. "Be safe," he says quietly. "Try to come home early."

Ted feels relieved that Maggie is passed out. Her crying or screaming in a drunken state is much worse on his nerves. It grows dark outside, but Ted never turns on the kitchen light. He sits quietly at the kitchen table for a long time.

## Essence of Family Addiction

Ten years have passed in the Jensen family since scene 1, and now Maggie is an active addict. Her husband and son share her anguish and losses. We refer to Ted and David as *co-addicts* because they suffer, too, in an addictive family system. Maggie's addiction is a wound that opens similar wounds in her spouse and son. Addiction contaminates the life of every family member. Although they all suffer, each feels terribly alone. The three members of the Jensen family feel more comfortable alone than together. Each has withdrawn from active involvement in the others' lives, and they use this indifference to protect themselves from further pain.

Addiction is an illness that destroys a person's ability to create and sustain meaningful relationships. Over time, everyone in an addictive family must adjust and adapt to profound psychological, emotional, and spiritual losses. No longer a family organized around mutual values, as was the Jensen family in part 1, the chemically dependent family is now organized around addiction. Family members who once found comfort, companionship, sustained love, and meaning with each other are now restless, irritable, and discontented.

Established routines such as coming home in the evening, sitting down for dinner, or getting children to bed have become unpredictable. Who will show up for dinner? Who will be drunk or high? Will Dad be angry, withdrawn, or giddy? Where will Mom be? Instead of being a place of refuge and sanctuary, home is now a place of uncertainty, danger, and pain.

## The Creation of Powerlessness

One of the key elements of addiction is powerlessness. No day at home ever seems the same. Not even dinner is predictable. As the addicted family member's disease progresses, she betrays every agreement and routine in the family. Because Dad has more and more hangovers, the children can no longer depend on him to prepare breakfast. Because Mom is dependent on Valium, the children can't rely on her to take them to the museum on Saturday mornings like she used to do. Because the adolescent daughter smokes dope and has become unreliable, the parents can no longer trust that she'll abide by curfews. No one can depend on anyone. Everyone is powerless to change the addict or control how the addiction affects the family.

In addiction, families are rarely able to act in their own best interest and exercise good choices. The addict is his own worst enemy and frequently makes poor decisions, a sign of the decay. The alcoholic who stops for a couple of quick bumps instead of going straight home as he had promised will lose real power that comes from self-esteem. He then compensates for this loss of authentic power by developing more *pseudo-power*, or false power. When the alcoholic finally goes home and is confronted, he may respond with anger, harsh words, lies, or intimidation. These tactics may help him win the argument, but they are based on pseudo-power, not authentic or ethical power. Using pseudo-power or intimidation lowers one's self-esteem and threatens the self-esteem of others in the family.

Because pseudo-power doesn't stem from the spiritual principles of betterment, it can't bring comfort to the person in the long run. Pseudo-power pushes people away, buries hurts and fears, and makes people tough and brittle at the same time. In a family operating under this type of power, children can't ask their parent a question without getting a defensive reply. Other family members may become cynical. They have faith in no one but themselves.

In addictive families, power struggles increase as the illness progresses. If more than one family member is addicted, one ego battles another; in families with a single alcoholic, one ego may battle many. Though decisions get made, no real solutions are achieved. Relationships and individuals get bruised and battered. Anger and arguing become commonplace. The addictive family becomes, as one man explains, "a bunch of warriors":

> We were warriors at war with each other. Someone would say hello and you answered back with anger or a groan. We never gave an inch. Giving in meant you were weak, a loser. We were dependent on our ability to react quickly and appear angry and powerful. I haven't lived with my family for years, but my wife said I still grunt out answers. She has nicknamed me Attila the Hun. Now she uses it affectionately, but my anger almost cost me my marriage.

Most humans react quickly and naturally when facing danger. When we see someone angry, his eyes dilated, skin reddened, we tense up, keep watch on the person, or react angrily ourselves. Survival instincts kick in. Sensing danger, we step into a defensive mode and prepare for attack. The addicted family is always surrounded by danger. Addiction itself is like a vicious animal continuously threatening the family. So the family is always alert, on guard, and threatened. On a preconscious level, family members sense the dangerous and fatal nature of addiction. Though denied by the addict and others, the illness is a tyrant who controls the family. It dictates how peaceful or stormy dinner will be, when the alcoholic returns from the bar, how frightened the children will feel at bedtime, or if the parent will wake up in time to help the kids off to school. No wonder addictive families are filled with frustration, anger, and shame. It's understandable that with such chaos and powerlessness at home, family members seek power to defend themselves. This kind of family depends on its defense systems to solve problems instead of its collective reasoning and communication. Much of the arrogance, self-righteousness, stubbornness, yelling, and crying that characterize the addictive family result from the misuse of power and the need to protect oneself.

Dynamic changes occur when a family acts less from ethical, authentic power and more from pseudo-power. Family members become more reactive, that is, they constantly scan for danger and, when they sense it, react to avoid or control it. Fear and conflict increase. Parents become less able to find solutions. Conversations are marked by expression of ego and use of tones, gestures, and intimidation. Anger is frequently used to "solve" problems. Meanwhile, powerlessness increases, frustrating each family member. Jack, the father of an eighteen-year-old crack addict, talks about how crazy he'd feel:

> I couldn't stand it anymore. Here was my son, the kid who used to cry if he couldn't be with daddy. Nothing I said mattered anymore. I was being forced to watch my son die before my very eyes— and to him there was nothing wrong! I got so mad. I would yell, scream, pound my fist, but nothing mattered. I didn't matter anymore. I felt defeated,

weak. It was very humiliating for a man like me
who had always got whatever he set his mind to.

Such reactions are normal within an addictive family.
The progression of the disease of addiction and the feelings
and experiences of family members follow a predictable
course, or set of stages.

Next we will explore the three stages of addiction.
Stage 1 is called the adjustment stage. It details how the
family adjusts to the presence of the addiction process. In
stage 2 the family members develop a protective persona,
which they use to protect and defend themselves against
the addictive process. Stage 3 is the hopelessness stage,
when family members finally despair. Understanding these
stages helps us identify where in the process of addiction
any family might be. Without intervention, family addiction will always progress through all three stages; however,
the addiction can be arrested at any stage.

# CHAPTER 3

# STAGE 1:
# ADJUSTMENT

Healthy families believe they'll go through life together. Of course, times of sorrow and difficulties may unsettle families, but rarely do families question their stability. In healthy families, members trust their connection to each other. They look out for each other, confront each other when needed, listen carefully, and offer support. Though this doesn't always happen, it happens a good percentage of the time.

In addiction, however, the intoxication experience seduces and lures the addict away from her family. This person becomes powerless to resist the pull of the drug or alcohol experience. Slowly or sometimes quickly, she drifts from her family values, routines, rituals, and beliefs. The addict creates an "alternative" family consisting of barroom friends, cliques, or gangs, which becomes more important than her immediate family. Getting high or loaded with street buddies, watching weekend football or basketball games in neighborhood sports bars with new pals, or spending hours alone in a bedroom smoking dope becomes a higher priority than the addict's spending time with children, spouse, siblings; going on a summer vacation; or completing Saturday morning household chores. In this first stage, the addict's circle of friends starts to become his primary relationships. His emotional ties and commitment are transferred from family, friends, and community to other addicts. Instead of depending on family support to work out issues, the addict now turns more and more to the addictive process. Faced with going to a drinking party with people he doesn't even know versus going out with good, long-term friends who don't drink, the addict now chooses the former more frequently. Addiction starts to dictate one's lifestyle, choices, and selection of friends. The addict or alcoholic uses alcohol or other drugs to relieve the stress and problems of the day. Instead of coming home and talking to his spouse after a bad day at work, he now stops for happy hour at the local bar. The daughter who used to come straight home from school and relax now heads to a friend's house to smoke dope. The addict is increasingly unavailable to the family.

In stage 1, the family begins to adjust and adapt to the continuous presence of the addiction. Everyone in the family now feels the painful effects of the addict's distancing herself from the family. However, the addict lives in denial and observes none of this. Though family members will press the addict for an explanation, the addict finds this concern an annoyance. Roger, a thirty-five-year-old client, recalls how annoyed he'd get at his wife's inquiries when he was a practicing alcoholic, husband, and father:

I'd get so upset. My wife would keep asking, "Why are you drinking so much more? What's with you? You seem to care more about that TV than you do us!" To me, she was crazy—I wasn't drinking more and if I was, so what? I deserved it. I worked hard. To me, *she* was the one who was changing. Her questions annoyed me. I started to see her as a nag and someone who just didn't like to have fun. I kept telling her to lighten up.

Roger's change of behavior and increased drinking would naturally prompt anyone to question him and expect a reasonable answer. Yet, Roger dismissed his wife's concerns. If he took her concerns seriously, he would have had to look at his drinking. To avoid this, he criticized her and called her a "nag." Roger, like any addict when questioned about his drug or alcohol abuse, simply tried to stop what threatened the intimacy of his most important relationship—the relationship with his drug of choice. Normally, when nonaddicts abuse alcohol and drugs and are challenged by a spouse, they will listen and change their behavior accordingly. Even for the occasional abuser of chemicals, truth and intimacy are more important than continued drug or alcohol use. Addiction, however, seems to blow psychological fuses. Any illumination or insight to one's self is blocked.

In the preceding example, when Roger brushed off his wife's concerns, he brushed *her* off. No wonder her fears and concerns increased. She saw her husband increasingly choose the meaning*less* route of addiction over the more meaning*ful* route of family. Rather than spending the evening in an intimate discussion with his wife, Roger chose to drink and watch television. If this had happened only once or twice, it might not have become a major problem or issue. But Roger's wife saw him repeatedly use television as another excuse to sit on the couch and drink. In effect, Roger assigned "meaning" to a meaningless activity by increasingly giving his valuable and limited time to drinking. His wife, who deeply loved him, watched him abandon true meaning for pleasure and make meaningless choices, and she was naturally concerned.

For the addict, a loved one's concern is a threat, and he responds to that threat by trying to minimize, rationalize, or attack the person's concerns. Because genuine loving concern is always spiritual in nature, the addict tries to distort it into something bad like "nagging." This reaction only makes the family more concerned. Remember, healthy family life is about meaning. In such a system, we monitor meaningful and meaningless choices that other family members make. If too many meaningless choices are being made, we feel scared. For example, parents of an addicted son may be frightened on hearing that their son will not return to college but instead move in with a friend who was recently arrested for drug possession. They express their concerns, hoping the son will listen and make different plans. When confronted, however, the son will likely become angry or defensive. Like any addict, he will see his reaction as natural, because he believes he is making good, meaningful choices.

## The Love No One Hears

Love is what traps family members in the addictive process. When they see their spouse, parent, or child using chemicals and making bad choices, harming their future, and reducing meaning and intimacy in their lives, they naturally rush in to help. Who wouldn't? This help, however, is not appreciated.

The addict brushes them aside. "Leave me alone!" she yells. "I'm not hurting anyone but myself." This reaction only makes family members worry more. Anxiety increases.

In this first stage, when addiction works its way into the family, anxiety is a "normal" feeling. Everyone adjusts to an ever-present level of tension at home. It is right for the family to feel anxious. Family members sense the danger and finality of addiction in their home, and as the addict continues to discount their concerns, they get more scared. Although she is confronted, the addict never sees or hears her family's love and concern.

Over time, daily family life usually becomes a power struggle. The addict locks horns with the co-addicts; each fights to prove the other wrong; each tries to win the other over. Kathy, the mother of a recovering addict, describes how the effects of such a power struggle can last "for years," even after the addict enters recovery:

> It was crazy. Here I was on Saturday night picking my daughter up at the hospital after she had been treated for an overdose. I'm scared to death and she is telling me not to worry! Did she think that would comfort me? With each word that came from her mouth, my stomach would tighten to the point where I couldn't stand it anymore. I yelled at her to shut up. I screamed, if she really wanted to help *me*, she'd get treatment for *herself*. This scared her and she yelled that she wasn't going anywhere that would brainwash her. What did she think all those drugs were doing? This was the first time I had to really start looking at the craziness that

invaded our home. I was scared. The fear lasted for years. In fact it has never left, even though she just got her pin for being three years sober. The fear has lessened, but it's still there, especially on Saturday nights.

## Trust Eroded

During the first stage of addiction, family members want to give the addict the benefit of the doubt, but often can't. Their instinct tells them different. Denise explains what it feels like to be caught in the double bind of wanting to trust yet mistrusting a loved one:

> He kept telling me there wasn't a problem—that it was the stress of his job that was getting in the way and that, yes, he had made some bad decisions around drinking but not to worry. The stress, he'd say, would be over soon, and he'd be more careful in the future. It sounded reasonable. He was under stress at work. He promised it wouldn't become a problem. He was saying what I hoped he would say, but there was something in the way he was saying it that didn't relieve my fears. He'd get angry when I looked at him with concern. "Why won't you trust me?" he'd yell.

Denise wanted to trust her addicted husband, but something inside told her not to. This angered her husband, and he reacted self-righteously. It filled him with questions: Who are they to doubt me? How dare they mistrust me? What makes them think they're any better? When family members display their mistrust, addicts also come to mistrust their families. Addicts feel suspicious and uncomfortable when they hear their family members' concerns.

Because the addict is constantly being manipulated by the intoxication experience and becomes manipulative himself, he views everyone else in the same light. It's impossible for him to see concern as genuine. He believes his loved ones are trying to trick him or force him to stop drinking or using. Consequently, to protect himself, the addict grows increasingly mistrustful and distances himself from the family. When family members see the alcoholic retreat and become more chemically dependent, they become even less willing to trust the addict.

Trust is essential in intimate relationships. Without trust, relationships will disintegrate. This means that a family must reestablish trust to survive. To do so involves confronting the addiction—which won't likely happen. Mom may come downstairs in the morning, apologize for her drinking and yelling the night before, and promise it will not happen again. Her spouse and children may accept her apology and pretend everything will be better, but they intuitively know that in a week or two another drunken episode will occur. Apologies no longer mend relationships; promises have become worthless, as all involved trust each other and themselves less and less.

## Addiction Starts to Govern

During the adjustment stage, the illness of addiction slowly distorts the interactions among family members. Addiction affects the family on four levels: behavioral, mental, emotional, and spiritual.

### Behavioral

As the addict's drug or alcohol use progresses, the person acts out more. Family members clearly see a problem in the addict's behavior. The wife cannot ignore the missed meals and late nights of drinking. The husband cannot ignore the empty whiskey bottle in the morning. The children cannot pretend that the fighting at home and the drinking aren't related. In stage 1, family members may not know, believe, or be willing to admit that the problem is addiction—but they know there's a problem. They know the drinking or drugging of a family member increasingly governs them. It is reflected in their minds, attitudes, and behavior. Each day, when the children come home from school, they wonder what awaits them on the other side of the door.

### Mental

More energy and time are now spent trying to understand what is happening. Everyone repeatedly relives the crazy fights. Family members may spend hours talking to each other or thinking to themselves, analyzing the addict's behavior. Everyone wonders why the son slams his fists into the bedroom walls; why Father is coming home in the morning just when the children are sitting down to breakfast; why Mother sneaks down to the basement every night after supper. The addict, too, wonders how he could have yelled those terrible things at everyone. His mental habits and reasoning change. The kids listen more attentively in health class when addiction is discussed. Spouses find their attention drawn to television shows on addiction. Everyone is asking why and searching for answers. In their drive for meaning, family members seek to make sense of what is fundamentally senseless.

### Emotional

The addict's comments are intended to steer family members away from defining her problem as addiction. She blames others for her destructive behavior: "It's your fault.

You pick on me too much. You're wrong. If you weren't such a nag, I'd come home." In this first stage of addiction, the addict creates a delusional defense system that allows the addiction to progress. Faced with the addict's attacks, family members naturally defend themselves, which only draws them into a meaningless battle with the addict. They may soon find themselves developing their own form of self-deception to put the problem out of their minds: "It's nothing. He doesn't drink that much. She'll be okay once she finds a job." Deep emotional changes occur in this stage. Divisions develop that may take years to heal. Blaming others gives the addict a psychological hiding place. Other family members hide in their own resentments. Gina, whose husband is five years sober, speaks of how her resentments let her escape looking at her own behavior:

> It is only in the last couple of years that I've started to get a handle on my resentments. They were the moth-eaten blankets I wrapped myself in when he was drinking. I always thought he created them; only now am I seeing that I created them. I still treat him as someone who can't be trusted, even though he has acted trustworthy for five years. His drinking was keeping us apart; now my resentments are keeping us apart.

### Spiritual

On the spiritual level, the addict is starting to betray principles such as honesty, hope, and respect of self and others. He doesn't realize that he's powerless over drugs or alcohol and deludes himself. The addict believes if he did not drink on an empty stomach, if he drank only wine and didn't mix it with beer, if he didn't drink until after supper, then he will be fine. The addict is moving *away* from a world organized around values and principles *toward* a world based on pleasurable sensations. At this point, addiction slowly takes control of the individual and the family. More and more time is spent trying to protect the addict or alcoholic. However, the addict continues to miss dinners; forgets he had promised to take his kids fishing on Saturday and stays in bed until noon nursing a hangover; passes out on the front lawn or nearly crashes the car while driving with the children in the backseat. No wonder addicts feel guilty just being around their families. The looks on the faces of their loved ones can cause addicts to feel intense shame. Anna hated the concerned "look" she would get from her children and husband:

> During my addiction I remember slowly drifting away from my family. I remember them, at first, trying to get me to do things, but distance from them felt good and meant I could use without feeling guilt. Often, when I spent time with them, they had *that look* that made me feel guilt. I started to feel angry when I would think of *that look*. I wanted less time with them and more time alone, which meant more time to use. Looking back, I knew I was betraying my agreement to be their mother and his wife, but at the time I blamed them and *that look* for the distance I created. After a while, everything I did revolved around getting high, and everything they did revolved around them trying to save me from myself.

## Avoidance and Control Replace Meaning

The family now operates more and more from drives of pleasure and power. Family members protect themselves by avoiding and minimizing the problems caused by addiction. A mother who finds drugs in her daughter's room convinces herself that the daughter is only going through a stage; a father may not see his son's two DWIs as a serious problem. "It could happen to any kid. It's bad luck," the father says.

In an attempt to fix problems at home, family members may try to control the addict. A wife might think that if she can get her husband to come straight home from work instead of stopping at the bar, everything will be okay. A father might hope that if he can help his son make it through baseball season and those drunken softball games, everything will be all right. But long after the baseball season ends, the illness keeps progressing, more fears are created, and his son continues drinking.

The more family members fear for the addict's life, the more they try to control that person. This is especially true in later stages of addiction. However, attempts to control the addict only push her further away, which in turn creates more fear. Addiction is a vicious circle, a serpent that loops back and bites its own tail.

Parents and children try to help the addict, but all attempts fail. Feeling frustrated and exhausted, family members may find refuge in their own anger and its sensations of power. The anger a father may feel when his alcoholic son comes home late protects him from feelings of powerlessness and loss that lie just below the surface. The drive for meaning is replaced by the drive for power that protects oneself from deeper, more vulnerable feelings.

When this happens, control is desired more than truth. The family system becomes control- or avoidance-centered.

Addiction is based on a false belief in control. The addict believes he can control the substance, and the family believes it can control the addict. When high, the addict believes he has found "the answer" that will provide the control he needs to ensure a good life for himself. Addicts often act as if they have all the answers. They think they have found an easier, softer way to become complete. Though they feel in control, especially in the beginning of their drug or alcohol use, they have become unsuspectingly addicted to a process whereby they lose control of their lives. They feel they have conquered the lion only because they can't see it anymore. In reality, they can't see it anymore because their heads are in the lion's mouth.

## The Family Becomes Reactive

When scared and in need of protection, we instinctively seek power. Although it is rarely the best solution, power distances us and makes us feel less vulnerable. This is important to understand. As the family sinks deeper into the addictive process, everyone's fear level increases and more "power" is sought for a defense. Human beings can't stand to feel powerless for prolonged periods of time. Someone scares us and we yell back, "What did you do that for?" It's the fight-or-flight reaction. Anger distances us from our own fear. Our drive for power is there to protect us. We stop feeling helpless. Imagine a parent pacing at five in the morning because his sixteen-year-old daughter is not home. The parent is frightened. But when the daughter straggles in, the parent puts aside his fear and yells, "Where the hell have you been?" A fight evolves. Family members naturally feel angry, resentful, and self-righteous in their attempts to stop feeling fear and powerlessness.

Also, in order to control the addict, family members may threaten or shame the addict: "You've ruined this family! You're the reason this family is falling apart!" Fearing that these statements may be true, the addict often reacts in a defensive, angry manner. Tony, an addict of many years, walked around shameful and defensive most of the time:

> During my addiction, any time my family commented on my using or even sounded like they might comment on my using, I reacted with anger and bitterness. It worked—it worked *well*. They would react, and within seconds, we'd be in a fight that would allow me to leave and go get high. When I used certain words and tones, I could feel myself puff up with self-righteousness and blame them for the problems we were having. I ran to my drive for power. I hid in it, and I bullied my family from it. Looking back, they would run to their drive for power for the protection it offered them and hold their own against this raging, out-of-control addict—me.

Addicted families, like Tony's, turn to the sensations that pseudo-power offers. But by seeking refuge in their drive for power—by using arguments and tactics similar to those of the addict—they play into the addictive process. As family members retreat deeper into themselves, they become collectively isolated.

Think of the addictive system as a *system of negative adaptation*. Family members will continue to adjust and adapt to the illness of addiction. It is like the pine bush growing high on the mountain whose growth is determined by the forces of the wind and elements. The bush does not grow straight because its life is a continuing reaction and adjustment to the elements on the mountain. Each of the curves and distortions of its branches reflects a relationship or battle it endured with the winds, cold, and rain. Its ability to stand there is a monument to its survival. Like the wind, addiction bends, twists, and threatens to break the limbs of the family itself.

## Living within a Double Bind

During stage 1 the entire addictive family begins living within multiple double binds. Members believe they have to fix the problem, yet they can't. Their heads tell them they're not to blame, yet in their hearts they believe they are. The addict wants to connect with the family, yet rejects the family in favor of her addiction. The family's concerns attract and repulse the addict. The addict wants more freedom to pursue her growing addiction *and* wants the family not to be upset.

The family's desires to help the addict are rejected. This hurts the family members and causes them to develop, like the addict, an internal defense system. If something regularly hurts us, we naturally find a way or style to defend ourselves. So, though the family genuinely cares about the addict, the members also want to avoid the addict. Each family member approaches the addict out of love *and* avoids the addict out of pain.

The family's defense system and care system, operating simultaneously, contradict each other. Any movement in one direction creates an internal reaction in the other. If out of self-protection you move away from the addict, you feel guilt; if out of love you move toward the addict, you feel scared. Family members are "damned if they do and damned if they don't." Listen to Bill's account of the double bind he felt with his alcoholic wife:

> I'd end up frozen. I knew she was in trouble and needed help but any—and I mean any—attempts to help her would mean dealing with the ugly side of her being. And could she get ugly! Just try to help her and the yelling would start. But then there were the other times when she would just come up to me and want to cuddle on the couch. I got so confused that whenever she did this, I'd tense up, and she'd get angry at me for tensing up. Inside, I felt like I could never do the right thing.

Bill, like most family members, ended up frozen like a deer in the headlights of addiction. He didn't know what to do: stand still or run for the woods.

## Dialogue to Monologue

During the adjustment stage, the family's style of communication undergoes a fundamental shift. Families that had communicated respectfully, listening to each other and sharing information, now find themselves defensive and in conversations that go nowhere. Discussing problems once led to solutions but now only collapses into arguments and debates. While family members once communicated to find out *what* was wrong, they now communicate to find out *who* is wrong.

Healthy communication is a dialogue wherein each family member is willing to be influenced by another. In every genuine conversation, the participants are mutually vulnerable. All parties are generally enriched by the conversation. Healthy dialogue layers information to build understanding. The successful placing of one layer on the next allows for more complex discussions. More problems get resolved. In dialogues, people *listen to* each other; in monologues, people *talk at* each other.

In healthy communication, participants listen for where the truth is and then move toward it. In the addictive family, on the other hand, truth poses a threat. If the family members talked about addiction openly, they could work toward a solution. However, because of his chemical dependence, the addict must sabotage the truth and the communication process. Often, the mere mention of drinking, drug use, or other addictive behavior provokes an intense reaction.

In addictive families, each member builds an emotional wall for protection. From behind these walls, they scream at each other, issue statements, make judgments, and determine who is wrong and who is right. No one really expects to be heard, so they shout at each other. At this stage, making your point is critical. This *monologue style* of communication is very damaging to the family. No one is respected. Cal was totally frustrated by the way his family communicated:

> I would be surprised if anyone in our family could repeat back to anyone what they just heard or even what they said. Words became bullets; we would shoot them at each other. Everyone's favorite phrase was, "You're not listening to me!" Of course we weren't—what would you expect with three practicing addicts in the house?

## The Addict Increasingly Attacks the Family

As addicts become more dependent, they genuinely wonder why they have distanced themselves from their families. Unable to face their addiction, they are puzzled by their own behavior but know that it has hurt their families. However, in their denial, they can't be honest. The alcoholic son is not going to say, "I pick fights with Dad so I can go leave the house and get high." That's too honest. So when the addicted teen sees his father looking concerned, he feels compelled to discount his parents. Genuine love and concern must always be discredited. It would be too threatening for an addict to acknowledge another person's concern. "Who is he trying to kid?" the addict might say, seeing her father. "He has never cared about me. What a phony!" Now the addict can act self-righteous, pick a fight, and run to a friend's house where she can get high. Kay explains how her husband, Matt, wouldn't allow anything nice to be said to him:

> It was crazy. It got to a point where I couldn't say, "I have a good day" without Matt saying, "What do you mean by that?" I couldn't understand. It was as if my love or interest in him was a hot iron pressed against his skin. He would react, get angry, and blame me for his discomfort. At the best times, he'd get shameful and start rambling on about what a bad person he was and that he would do better. There was no way to love him. I think this was what was hardest on me. I started to ask myself, "What's wrong with me? What's wrong with my love?"

Kay brings up a good point. The addict's bouts of self-pity and promises to change actually undermine the health of the family. The addict's promises become painful to hear over and over. If the addict is encouraged to get help, she then verbally attacks: "I told you I would change. Isn't anything good enough for you? I told you I was sorry—now leave me alone!"

The addict projects his negative side onto his family members. Feeling guilty about getting drunk the night before, the alcoholic may walk downstairs in the morning, see the kids' toys on the floor, and start yelling at them for creating a mess. Others become "the villains." They are to blame. The energy that would normally be channeled into self-reflection, healing, and growth is now channeled into anger, hurt, and denial, which only intensifies the problem. The daughter who feels bad about her poor grades (due to her drug use) now argues and tells her parents that she never cared about grades in the first place. Her grades only mattered to her parents, she yells. She is not consciously attacking her parents, but unconsciously protecting herself. Remember, addiction is an unconscious process of negative adaptation. It makes the addict more and more comfortable to live in denial. The addict is playing by unfair rules. She can say and do whatever she wants.

In a power-centered family, the person with the most options possesses the most power. Subsequently, the addict—who is willing to risk more than anyone in the family—generally holds the most power. The co-addict (person or persons most directly connected to the addict) often counters the addict's power by getting angry and resentful. Sometimes this person appears more upset and unstable than the moody addict. Children may, in their fright, seek refuge in the port that appears calmer—the addict. This may anger the co-addict even more, so he in turn works to convince the children how crazy the addict is; what the co-addict doesn't realize is that the children already know this. The co-addict's anger, rage, sadness, depression, and resentments may actually force the children to choose the addict over him. This is how the children are often left with no real safe haven. They must now begin to parent themselves or each other.

## The Family Monitors the Addict

In this first stage of addiction, the addict's family begins monitoring him in a different way. The family is increasingly worried and concerned. Although this is natural, family members can be consumed by it.

Out of love, they try harder to stay connected by constantly checking up on the addict. After work, one father I knew would follow his daughter, a heroin addict, and watch her on the street. This is called "pursuing the addict." It normally develops toward the end of the adjustment stage. Although they have the addict's best interests at heart, when family members chase after the addict, he only gets more defensive and becomes verbally or physically abusive.

As family members spend more and more time scrutinizing their loved one who is in danger, they expend the energy that would normally be used to monitor themselves or family activities. The daughter who loves baseball stops going to games and comes home right after school to check on her alcoholic mother. The wife involved in town politics skips evening meetings in order to stay more connected to her addicted son. Again, this is normal, not abnormal.

Listen to Eddie talk about how his family made many sacrifices and spent endless hours monitoring him because they were afraid he might hurt himself:

> They were all over me. One little overdose and now every move of mine was watched. I couldn't be in my room alone without someone looking in on me every five minutes. My little brother was the worst. He wanted to be with me all the time. He

followed me everywhere. I would yell at him, and he would still follow me. I had to beat him up, and good, in order to get him to leave me alone. In treatment, I found out he was the one who had found me in my room turning blue with a needle hanging from my arm. He saved my life! Yet I had beat him up. That's what I had become.

The family, especially in this adjustment stage, becomes hyperalert for any clues or signs of trouble with the loved one. The co-addict still believes he can solve the problem and change the addict. Concerned family members may now set aside their personal needs for the immediate ones of the addict. Money needed to pay bills may now be used for the addict's car repairs. They lose sleep, worrying about where the addict is. Parents put lots of energy into helping their children get out of troubles, maybe driving three hundred miles to bail a son out of jail. These parents who think their son will be grateful, willing to listen to advice, and able to do what is best will be disappointed. After the crisis is over, family members may feel upset and ripped off. The alcoholic casts them aside, after a brief period of regrets. It is a mistake to assume that an addict will be grateful for your help. Ginny, a thirty-four-year-old mother, recounts her story of trying to help her son:

> God knows how many times we helped our son out. The first few times he seemed to be truly thankful. He listened as we talked about what we felt needed to happen for this problem to be solved. Back then, he would try to change and do better for a period of time. In time, however, he acted as if we were obligated to help him. If we showed any hesitation, he'd get furious and blame us for his

troubles. Back then, I believed it was my fault; after all, I was his mother. So I would monitor him more and more. He didn't know it, but sometimes I would follow him in the car and see where he was going. I discovered many crack houses in our town. It was as if my well-being was tied to his well-being; the more he hurt, the more I hurt. The scarier his life got, the more fear I would feel. At times, I would pray that I wouldn't care so much. It was as if my care, my love for him, was pulling me under and I was drowning. That's how crazy it got.

## How Children Are Affected

In chapter 7 we'll discuss in depth how family addiction affects children. It's important to mention at this point, however, a few notes about attachment needs for children during the first stage of addiction. Being vulnerable, children need a parent or parents for guidance and support. In the addictive family, however, where one or both parents are chemically dependent, children are faced with attaching to someone who feels dangerous to them. They want intimacy and support from their parents, but may at the same time be repulsed by them. For example, a child in an addictive system may desperately want to eat breakfast with her father, but knowing he may be hungover and in a bad mood, the child arrives at the breakfast table wearing emotional armor.

In addictive families, children's desires for attachment and intimacy also conflict with their own survival needs. When their attachment and intimacy needs go unmet time and time again, they come to believe that they need no one. Steve's example demonstrates the fierce ambivalence children can experience over an addicted parent:

I loved my mother dearly; in fact, I wanted to find a woman like her—that is, until her drinking got crazy and embarrassing. I remember the day my mother died inside of me. I walked into the house after school to find her passed out on the floor with her dress all bunched up around her waist and her underwear exposed to the world. She had urinated all over herself and the floor. I was so glad none of my friends had come home with me. I never brought anyone to my house after that. She had been a woman with much charm and style, and there she was looking so cheap.

In time, children like Steve solve their conflict by emotionally shutting down. Children can sense the danger in an addictive family and often know before the parents that something is terribly wrong. They know the family is not solving problems and is no longer as powerful (in a healthy way) as other "normal" families. In order to adapt, children may take the role of parents and provide for the emotional needs of the family. In an intact nuclear family with more than one child, children may have to divide up or take sides. If an adult addict in the family needs a friend, often a child must become one. If the spouse needs someone to reassure him, a child is there to offer support. If the parent needs someone to complain to, a son or daughter becomes available. With so many demands, children are forced to take sides in the family's political game. Parents campaign for support. Their speeches determine who is right and who is wrong. Each child gets only one vote.

As a parent's sense of failure increases, the children may rally and assume responsibility for building up their mother's or father's self-esteem. If sides have been drawn, children often believe they must put one parent down in their effort to support the other. This is why many children in addictive families feel they can have only one parent. Pam describes this problem and how she and her brother took opposite sides.

> My parents were at odds for as long as I can remember. Mom hated Dad for his using and the craziness that he got into, but we knew she would never leave him. My brother, Rick, was assigned to Dad and I to Mom. I would have to comfort her and shore her up; this meant going out with her on shopping trips that were designed to anger and get even with Dad. I got many nice clothes out of the deal, but I lost a lot of respect for my mother as well. You could tell what side I was on and what side Rick was on by our clothes. Mine were nice and current, and Rick's were old and ratty looking. I think one of the bigger costs to me was not getting to know my father and my brother. In my family, the two sides were not allowed to meet. It wasn't until treatment that I sat down and had a serious talk with my brother. We're a bit closer now, but the rules of addiction still seem to have a lot of power over us.

Children like Pam and Rick growing up in addictive families must often parent their own parents and provide them support and companionship. Although this may also happen in healthy families, healthy parents limit how much their children can help. "You're right," a father may say to his son. "I'm not okay, but it's not your job to fix me. Mom and I will solve this, not you. But thank you for noticing. You don't miss a thing." The parent will send the child off to play with a wink and a smile. These parents know that children are dependent and will forgo their needs for their parents. This is partly why parents must take care of themselves. It frees their children. When a child senses that his parents are doing well, the child is free to explore the world based on his own needs, not his parents' needs. Instead of monitoring his parents' world, the child is free to play and explore his own.

Children in this adjustment stage often wish to be older than they are. (Children do this in all families, but it occurs more frequently in the addictive family, and the desire is more intense.) Included within the wish to be older is the longing for power, which children often see as a solution. Being older and bigger means more power, and having more power means they can help save their families. Might can make right. As a boy, Eddy dreamed of power:

> I kept a scrapbook of all the famous and powerful people I would see in the magazines. I would love to sit and go through my scrapbook and dream of what I would do when I controlled the world. In my dreams I was a hundred feet tall. When I had all the power, I would kill all the drug dealers. [Eddy's mom was a heroin addict.] This was my favorite fantasy. I would make them all sit in the middle of the town and shoot up enough drugs so they would all die. God, how I longed to be big and powerful. Mom would be knitting on the sofa and I would sit on the floor next to her pasting pictures in my scrapbook. I dreamed of the days when things would be different. I guess my scrapbook was my drug of choice.

Eddy imagined power would enable him to save his mother. His fantasy to kill drug dealers shows that he knew addiction was a life-and-death matter. It's also important to know that desire for power grows in direct proportion to the powerlessness a family member feels. Loss of control intensifies the desire to gain control.

## Summary of How the Addictive Process Affects the Family

STAGE 1—ADJUSTMENT

| | |
|---|---|
| **Effects on Communication:** | Conversations shift from dialogue to monologue. |
| | Communication shifts from what is wrong to who is wrong. |
| | Addiction distorts communication and becomes a defense mechanism to protect the addictive process, which is getting established. |
| **Effects on Family Interaction Patterns:** | The addict emotionally creates distance from the family. |
| | Addiction disrupts rituals, routines, values, and beliefs that support the family. |
| | Co-addicts pursue and monitor the addict in an attempt to reconnect him or her to the family. |
| | The family starts the process of negative adaptation. |
| **Emotional Effects on Family:** | General feelings of anxiety increase. |
| | The family wants to trust the addict, but trust is constantly being eroded. |

Fig. 7

## CHAPTER 4

# STAGE 2:
# DEVELOPMENT
## OF A
# PROTECTIVE
# PERSONA

In this stage, family members usually develop a persona, or image, to protect themselves against the pain that addiction now regularly creates. The persona is like a suit of armor that shields the family from the blows of addiction. The mother of an addicted daughter who sobbed and cried for her daughter to change in stage 1 may become tough as nails, seemingly heartless, and stern in stage 2. This persona, or role, protects the mother from feeling more and more hurt. The emotionally strong husband who had acted decisively in the adjustment stage now becomes indecisive to protect himself from being attacked. The child who was once alert and active at school becomes a couch potato in response to the continuous chaos of his drunken parents. The stern mother, indecisive father, and lazy child are all personas that mask fear. When people live in an addictive family and face increasing problems, it's natural to develop such a persona. As the addict's ego grows, everyone must adapt. Some run and hide; some whistle in the dark and deny that anything has changed; others are like David challenging Goliath. For defense and emotional survival, family members put on personalities like costumes to protect themselves from further hurt.

In time, these costumes become like skin, real flesh. Family members mistake their personas for their true identities. They change their behavior and can't stop or return to being the authentic selves they were before the disease gained control over their family. Ned details how his persona protected him from his alcoholic wife *and* trapped him into being someone he wasn't:

> The worst part of my wife's addiction to sleeping pills was not watching her become someone I couldn't stand, but watching myself become someone I couldn't stand. She'd get high, and I'd feel weak and powerless to do anything. Instead of admitting this, I would yell and scream at her to grow up. Here I was stomping around screaming at the top of my voice for her to grow up, knowing all the while that I was out of control and weak next to her addiction. The only time I didn't feel weak was when I would puff myself up with anger, self-righteousness, and disgust for her.

Ned's enraged persona protected him from the helplessness he felt. Yelling and puffing himself up with anger made him feel superior and in charge. He could convince himself that he knew the right thing to do. These false beliefs came packaged with his persona. They developed in reaction to the meaning and ethical power being lost. As family members like Ned try to acquire more control, they act hard and tough with each other.

## The Decay of Ethical Power

When we strive for meaning in our lives, truth guides and directs our relationships and interactions. In the addictive family, truth means facing the addiction and becoming committed to recovery. *Denial* can be simply defined as turning away from the truth.

In the second stage of family addiction, family members become less and less committed to each other. They take fewer walks with each other. Picnics are unheard of now. Connection threatens one's emotional well-being. As this persona stage progresses, rugged individualism becomes the norm. The drives for power or pleasure are foremost in everyone's mind; meaning is secondary.

With this shift of priorities, or drives, the power base of the family also changes. Returning to Rollo May's five types of power (page 33) we see that it's now common for addictive families who once possessed what May calls "integrative" power—which binds and holds family members together—to descend to being "exploitative" of other family members. The family no longer lives and operates by ethical power but rather pursues the sensations of raw power. The most dominant person in the family, usually the addict, possesses the most force and now tries to exploit and manipulate others to accept her desires.

As the family disintegrates, the members lose faith in each other and now depend solely on themselves for survival. Daniel had found comfort and love in his family until addiction changed it radically:

> My family was the safest, most comfortable bunch of folks you would ever want to meet. We are now the most dangerous group of animals you could imagine, at least when we get together. We were once a team, and now a demolition derby. And what would you expect with three of six siblings being practicing addicts? We fight and use each other in any way we can. My brother even paid our little sister Rachel to deliver drugs to some of his customers, because if she was caught, she'd have no real consequences, since she's only fourteen.

Daniel knows firsthand how addiction turns healthy integrative families into exploitative ones, where the family members turn into predators, preying not only on others but on themselves as well.

## The *Why* Breaks Down

If an individual, couple, or family has a *why*, then the *how* of life becomes easier. The "why we are together" helps them through tough times: "We are together because we love each other. We work on relationships because we are a close family. We want to create a family because we want to nurture another life. We stay with each other out of choice, not necessity." The *why* of a family defines the group's purpose. Family members feel relieved and comforted if the *why* of their spiritual existence is honored and fulfilled. Why couples or families stay together is determined in their drive for meaning. We can stand the suffering that life gives us if we can find meaning in it. Meaning helps us transcend suffering. The ability to find meaning and purpose in life, however, dissolves under addiction's grip. The addictive process slowly disconnects a person from truth and prohibits the transformation of suffering into deeper understanding. Addiction is less transformative than accumulative. One hurt after another piles on top of each other.

As addiction progresses in stage 2, families and couples have a difficult time remembering why they are together. In the beginning, why a couple wanted to marry and start a family was easily answered: They loved each other. When addiction progresses, creating despair, frustration, and resentment, a different set of questions gets asked:

- Why did I ever marry this person?
- Why don't I just leave?
- Why am I a member of this family?
- Why can't I have different parents?
- Why is this happening to me?

In the addictive family, there are no answers, only frustration. Trish grew up in an alcoholic family, and many of her relatives still drink. She remembers the pain and frustration from asking unanswerable questions:

> For years I asked myself questions like, "What did I do to deserve being a member of this family?" Why me? It wasn't fair! I did everything I could not to be a member of my family. I wanted a normal family, to do normal things like family vacations, picnics, all the "fuzzy things" you heard that families do. At our last family picnic, two drunken uncles ended up in a fistfight, with one of them getting a broken jaw. All I could do was look to the heavens and ask, Why me?

When addictive families or couples lose their reason for existence, they work to *stay together* instead of *be together*. Family members actively look for reasons not to spend time together and develop separate lives as a way to buffer their losses. Without a *why*, they become a shame-bound family—a group of people who feel alone together.

## Decay of Love

In this second stage, the addictive family can no longer live according to the principles of betterment. The love starts to fall apart. Remember, love is made and held together by spiritual principles. If the family is now living within an environment that disconnects individuals from these principles, then creative love regresses into formless love. Such love lacks the power to influence and direct. Martha thought her love alone could cure her daughter's addiction. However, she had stopped being a mother and had become a coconspirator in the name of love:

> I never have and never will love anyone or anything more than Amy. She is the sweetest and most wonderful gift I have ever received. I thought my love alone would cure her addiction. She'd come home after a night of drinking and would be sick. I would hold her and tell her it would be all right. She would need money, and I gave it to her just to keep the sickness away and keep her tied to me and my love. But all this love meant little to her illness; it just kept taking more and more of her away from me. Thank God for treatment and that counselor who taught me to see that my love was killing my daughter. That counselor also showed me that my love had become words and not actions. My

actions were being controlled, not by love, but by my daughter's addiction. Love alone can't cure cancer, nor can it cure addiction. It was accountability, self-respect, and limits that helped my daughter find a home in recovery.

## Communication Worsens

Because we are social creatures, language and communication skills are fundamental to us. Language connects us with others; it implies relationships. Communication has two main functions: first, to connect with others; and second, to resolve issues and problems.

Listening is a vital part of communication. Through listening, we honor others, come to know them better, and learn from them. We increase our own knowledge base as we hear about and learn from others' experience. Because honest communication could lead to confrontation of the addiction, communication is always sacrificed in the addictive family.

Family members don't listen to each other; they only react. In this reactive mode, a person hears only the tones and the first few words of a conversation. Then, the person retreats into a protective persona and develops counterarguments. This causes communication to shut down. Isolation increases. Each family member grows lonely inside and, inevitably, feels dishonored by not being heard. In time, they know less and less about those who are foremost in their hearts. Rick describes his family's poor communication skills:

> Before coming to treatment, I think the last time I really listened and heard what someone else was saying was about ten years ago. I became so reactive and defensive that by the time Anna, my wife,

or anyone had finished their first sentence, I had my counter-argument set in my head. Certain subjects were not allowed. Drug use was one of them. I was rough on my family if they tried to break this rule. I would use my verbal talents as a salesman to make them feel stupid. I knew their weak spots and wouldn't think twice about using them. Anna's father had died when she was three, and I often used this wound to make her feel as if she was the wrong one. Questioning me about my drug use was only her way to get back at her father for dying. If she wanted me to stick around, maybe she should care a little bit about how I felt and my needs. I used this line of reasoning, or attack, if she got too close. After a while, she just stopped talking to me. We lived in the same house, but a million miles separated us.

In addictive families like Rick's, conversations are filled with ambiguity. As quarreling increases, communication becomes indecipherable. "I love you. Can't you act right?" a mother might say. "You're the best son a mother could ask for. Will you ever bring your grades up?" Communication is also dangerous. Escape routes are necessary for sharing to occur: "Yes, you're right. I did that, but if you hadn't . . . ." "I'll see you Thursday, if I can make it." "Of course I love you, especially if you would . . . ."

Most members of the addictive family become dominated by impulses. They tend to act out their feelings instead of talking them out. A young boy may act out his anger about his sister's drug use by going into her room and ripping the heads off her doll collection. He hopes that she gets the message. What he does not do and is unable to do is share his feelings with anyone in the family.

The problem of communication in the addictive system develops because the family is power-centered. Disguising your message is a way to keep power; if you can't be pinned down, then you can't lose.

## Anger as Protection

In the second stage of family addiction, anger becomes a primary defense for family members. "You can't hurt me because I don't give a damn" is a phrase often heard in these families. Indifference and apathy are viewed as sanctuaries.

When family members feel hurt or frightened, they reach for anger as if it were a weapon to defend them against danger. In the addictive family, individuals are regularly exposed to hurts and fears. Anger offers an asylum from those more vulnerable feelings. However, anger inevitably consumes those who seek refuge in it. Henry used his anger to keep the concerns of his family at bay:

> Each night as I walked up the sidewalk, I would put on what I called my hate face. That was my persona. I would think of all the things that I might find when I walked through that door. I'd try to remember everything people had yelled and screamed at me. I would not walk through that door until my mask of hate was on. Even if I had been having a good time earlier, I would sometimes walk around the block until the rage was boiling inside of me. It worked well; it got to the point that when I walked in the door, the family would see me, turn, and go the other way. No one dared to confront me about my drug use. They knew how ugly I could become.

It's not just the addict who becomes an expert at anger. Often the primary co-addict appears angry each time he is rejected, put down, or put off by the addict. Nonaddicts can't escape into a drug high, so their defenses must become stronger, thicker. It's not uncommon for children in addictive households to report that the "other" parent was more angry than the addicted one. Ginny remembers growing up with an alcoholic father and angry mother:

> My mom had a mouth. Dad would come home happy, half in the bag, and she was all over him. We felt sorry for him. We excused his drinking and blamed Mom and her temper. It wasn't until treatment, seeing Mom break down and cry for two days straight, hearing her talk of dreams and plans gone bust due to the drinking, did I start to understand the anger. I was so busy dealing with it, I never looked behind it.

Swearing, vulgarity, and yelling are expressions of anger. They also serve as defenses or masks, a way of appearing tough and in control. These defenses allow one to feel powerful quickly; this is not true power. Foul language actually diminishes the speaker and is a form of psychic violence, a verbal club. As the family breaks down, words and communication also break down. Swearing is a sign of this spiritual breakdown.

## Survival Replaces Intimacy

During this second stage of addiction, family members often give up on intimacy. They perceive intimacy and expressions of love as dangerous and no longer worth the effort. Because they are using all their energy for survival, intimacy seems like fluff, extraneous and unreliable. It also threatens their tough exterior and so is quickly for-saken for the armor of a protective persona. Again, fami-ly members develop such personas because they believe they are on their own.

As the addiction becomes more central in the day-to-day lives of the family members, they experience a subtle shift in attitude. The alcoholic stops acting as though he even likes his wife. He may openly flirt with other women at parties. He tells himself that it's okay because his own wife rejects him sexually. He doesn't understand that she might be repulsed when he comes home drunk, smelling of booze and cigarettes, and falls on top of her. He sees him-self as Casanova, not as a smelly, pushy, overbearing person. Others in the family begin to act similarly, ignoring each other and being less available. Their protective masks now seem more real and authentic than their true selves.

Survival is a priority. Parents and children no longer suspect that alcoholism and drug addiction is the prob-lem—they know it is. This is their everyday reality. Daily family life becomes a burden. For the children, home is a place to avoid, and school now the place to relax or the place where they act out the frustrations of home. Home is a place to run from, not a place to return to.

## Family Becomes Polarized

As previously mentioned, the addictive family often breaks down into camps. In this way, a family member can at least keep ties with one or two others. The addict and her supporters are often on one side; the co-addicts on the other side. Often subcamps are made within the co-addict's side.

Often, one set of co-addicts believes control is needed and boundaries must be made and respected. "If this thing is going to get turned around, someone has to take the bull by the horns and face the problem head on," a co-addict might say. Another set of co-addicts supporting the addict believes everyone should lighten up and relax. "We are too tough on her," one might say. Although both views are valid, the solution lies in weaving them together. But as camps form and sides get taken, brothers find themselves pitted against sisters, one parent against another. A son who believes care will fix the problem is speaking from his own feelings of hurt and loneliness. A daughter who seeks to control the addict speaks from her own scared and panicked feelings.

Power struggles develop between the camps. Each side feels more frightened and more justified as it considers the course suggested by the opposite side. The "control side" fears a tactic based on understanding and care, knowing that the addict will use such treatment to take more from the family. The "care side" fears confronting the situation, knowing how angry and mean the addict can get; the family members on this side want to avoid provoking at all costs. Russell reports on the great debates about what to do with his sister:

> We would spend hours sitting in a room arguing about what to do with Sherry. We talked and talked. People would get afraid and stop listening. Voices would rise. Most often, it became a shouting match. Each of us clearly believed that we had "the" solution to Sherry's addiction. What we were talking about was the pain and fear that we all felt. We were so beat up and scared! Eight years with a sister in and out of detox and treatment inflicts a lot of pain. You couldn't look at her without

getting afraid. She always looked near death. For each of us, our pain was the true energy, the true demons, behind those doors. One day the discussions just stopped. No one wanted to sit and talk anymore. The talking that went nowhere hurt as much as looking at Sherry.

Russell's story illustrates how later in this stage of addiction the debates become useless. The camps break up and the family members drift apart.

## Distancing

In the addictive family, distancing becomes a form of self-care. It's natural to distance from pain, especially when one is powerless to eliminate it. Accordingly, stage 2 is when each family member sets up a *parallel life*. Siblings and even parents go outside the family to find relationships that will meet their needs, which are not being met within the family. Living a separate life that no one in the family is aware of brings a kind of hope, a place for self-esteem, and a chance for intimacy. The family has become a burden, and the antidote is seen as independence or artificial families, such as gangs and drinking clubs. As individual family members invest more and more into their "other lives," they may indeed find some relief, but it is often accompanied by an underlying sense of guilt for abandoning the family. Also, since these individuals are taking their fear of intimacy out into the world with them, they often fail to connect with others. Below we see how Grace looks for freedom through the pursuit of her own independence:

I saw and still see independence as my goal. Watch

your own back because no one else will. This is my self-care. I was and still am my own best friend. Having extra time on my hands doesn't scare me; in fact, I enjoy being by myself with nothing to do. Time goes by quickly. I had a couple of people who have wanted to get close to me and it just never works out. I get nervous if I have to spend too much time with just one person. I kidded my family that I think I could get married if I could live in a separate house from the person I would marry.

For Grace, independence is a blessing and a curse. It saved her from the hurt and fear of growing up in an alcoholic family but now keeps her from developing more mature and intimate relationships.

## Family Rituals Break Down

One of the ways families create closeness is through rituals. Rituals, including daily dinners, evening card games, and more celebratory occasions like Christmas, birthdays, or family reunions, help us reconnect and recommit. Rituals pull family members together during difficult times. For example, a wake and funeral following the death of a loved one can support a family in its grief.

Since rituals create intimacy and connection, addictive families quickly find their long-standing routines and rituals disrupted and polluted. An alcoholic family member may get drunk, fall into the Christmas tree, and ruin a ritual your family has followed since your childhood. The heroin addict may fail to show up at his brother's birthday party. Thanksgiving dinner now includes tears and disappointment. The addict acts out and spoils the joy of holidays, birthdays, anniversaries, or even simple routines like Saturday trips to the woods that once brought joy and comfort. After a while, individual members and eventually the entire family abandon the rituals. Certain family members make other plans for Christmas or other holidays. Trish remembers how this happened in her family:

> About two or three times a week, after supper, we'd all get together to play cards. We would catch up on all the news, laugh, make fun of each other, and have fun doing it. When Dad's alcoholism got worse, he stopped playing and only drank instead. While playing cards, we heard the car pull up the drive, and all of us in the room got quiet. When the door was opened, you could hear a pin drop. We'd look over to see which Dad was walking through the door: the sober one or the drunk. If it was the drunk, we'd all quickly leave the table. Becky, my little seven-year-old sister, said it was easy to tell which Dad was home: "Just look into his eyes. You can see if Dad is home or the other guy is there." After a while the card games just stopped.

Rituals that created love, fun, connection, and happiness in Trish's family were destroyed by alcoholism.

## Negative Happiness

Addicted families define happiness as a lack of crisis, by what does not happen. When a day or a week goes by without a fight at home, it is marked on a person's psychological calendar. If Dad doesn't stumble and cut open his chin on the stairs, if Mom doesn't shout at everyone during dinner, if brother Billy doesn't stay out past eleven on a school night, or if sister Sue doesn't cry herself to sleep, then everyone is happy. This is negative happiness. It is about protection, a way to continue to care but not too much. It speaks to how long the family has lived under the shadow of addiction.

In stage 1, when the nineteen-year-old son comes home and passes out on the front lawn, it's a crisis. Everyone talks about it in the morning. "This is crazy," a sibling may say. "We have to get him help." Then, three years later, in stage 2 of addiction, when the same son comes home and again passes out on the front lawn, everyone is happy to see him. At least they know where he is. At least they know he's safe and not dead in a car crash somewhere. At least the parents and family members get to care for him, love him, before his addiction takes him away again. This negative happiness brings some "comfort" to family members.

Family members, however, don't count on anything good or positive coming their way. They take their daily dose of pain, sometimes even inflict it on themselves as a vaccine against a larger dose they'll likely receive when the addicted person comes home. A teenager might find herself relaxing, but then remember the fight her mom and dad had the night before. The teen doesn't want to lose her edge and become too relaxed and trusting. Cynicism becomes a way to protect against disappointment. Some even think it keeps them happy. Eighteen-year-old Betty describes how an alcoholic may define happiness:

> I'd be nice and sweet if that's what someone wanted; I'd be mean and nasty if that's what the situation called for. The one thing I couldn't be was real, my genuine self. My happiness became the satisfaction of running a good scam, keeping people off my back, and winning a good fight. I felt happy when I knew no one could touch me. I'm embarrassed to admit it now, but one of my "happiest" events was when I was out late one night

with a couple of friends, and we ran across a homeless drunk. I started yelling, pushed him down,
ended up kicking and punching him until my
friends got scared and pulled me off. The story
spread through school, and a lot of kids were even
more afraid of me. Little did they know I was
punching and kicking my alcoholic parents. I now
do volunteer work at a homeless shelter—my Al-
Anon sponsor's idea—as a way hopefully to forgive
myself someday for beating that man senseless.

Members of addictive families want happiness as much
as anyone else; they just don't trust it. They're afraid to
become invested in it. For the addictive family, happiness is
a liability. For some, like Betty, making others suffer is more
thrilling than making others happy.

## The Victim Persona

Not all family members develop a tough persona as Betty
did. Some take refuge in the persona of the victim.
Addiction, like any major illness, victimizes the diseased
individual *and* the addict's family members.

Without support, family members feel as if they're constantly under siege. They never know what waits for them
at home: a passed-out parent, an angry, abusive sibling, or a
trip to the emergency room with a gash in Mother's head
from a drunken fall. Family members become victims, afraid
to relax and let their guard down. Hypervigilant, each is a
soldier on sentry duty in a combat zone. Something seems
to be out there; the question is, Will it get you?

Although the victim persona would seem to offer a
good defense, it is very destructive. It robs individuals of
choice, and in so doing traps them inside a wound created

by someone else. Anna had established an identity as a victim of her mother's addiction:

> Boy was I a victim. I was an expert in suffering. I loved to tell my friends about the things I had to put up with at home just to hear them say, "Oh, that sounds horrible. You must be a strong person to put up with all that." I would get furious if any-one tried to point out options or things I was doing that were making it worse: "They don't understand. How insensitive! If only they knew." I resisted help. In family treatment I kept yelling, "It's not my fault! It's them! Get them off my back." I thought the counselors were the meanest people. I thought their work must have warped them permanently, though all they were trying to do was help me see that I had choices. I had become afraid of choices. I felt that I always made the wrong choices, for if I hadn't, Mom would have stopped taking drugs. It wasn't till I faced that I was trapped more by my own shame and beliefs that I started to step out from behind the empty protec-tion that being a victim offered me.

Anna, like many children growing up in addictive fam-ilies, had come to fear choices. Often teens feel they must either put up with the addiction or leave. A younger child has only one of these options.

## Crises Become More Regular

Every family experiences crises, which are points in time where decisions get made and directions forged, ideally toward solutions. In addictive families, however, crises occur frequently and rarely produce solutions or growth. At times, they may even be created simply to release pent-up emotions and tension. Tobias recalls how he intentionally created crises with his father just to release tension:

> Looking back at my family, I would say that I worked with Dad to create a crisis and allow everyone to vent. I know that sounds strange, but I could tell when Dad was in one of those moods. There would be a quietness that had a danger attached to it. It was like that ugly green quiet the sky gets right before a storm. It was then my job to do something to set him off. I would drop a glass and break it, leave something in his path, anything—it didn't have to be much—and he would go off on me. He'd hit me, scream at me, and push me around until the whole family was crying, screaming, and acting like the sky was falling. I think it had to be me, because the other kids were too afraid of him. I also had my own dope to lessen the impact of the blows. I hated him, but I wasn't that afraid of him.

Intentionally or not, Tobias and his father worked together to give the entire family an opportunity to release emotions. This does not make Tobias responsible for his father's abuse, but it does illustrate how a family system regulates and develops different roles and personas, often depending on the emotional strengths and weaknesses of its members.

## New Rules Get Created

Some families try to gain control over escalating crises by developing more rules. This is especially true when the addict is an adolescent. The rules are attempts to control. When a crisis happens, someone comes up with a plan to control the situation and stop the crisis. The addict who caused the upheaval often agrees with the new rules, which causes others to momentarily back off. Everyone relaxes a bit as the addict signs the new rule, though with disappearing ink. Making rules is a coping mechanism used to decrease the family's tension. It often signals a temporary end to a crisis. Sonia agreed to hundreds of rules, none of which she followed:

> It went like this: I would go out and get crazy and scare them. I would then have to sit and listen to the *When Are You Going to Change* lecture. I might be high on dope, but I would listen respectfully. Sometimes, I would break down and tell them how very sorry I was. I'd promise I would stop acting so crazy. The next step was theirs. They would come up with a theory of what was wrong and develop a new rule to solve the problem. I would listen, pretend to be excited about the new rule. The only time I resisted one of their rules was when Mom, after she started to go to Al-Anon, said if I used again, it was treatment or move out of the house. Breaking this rule ended up with me in treatment.

## Shame and Blame

As previously mentioned, the addictive system is shame-based. Shame results, in part, because everyone knows on some level that the family isn't thriving and each person is somehow contributing to this condition. Shame is hard to live with. It makes us feel worthless and self-loathing. Rather than deal directly with one's shame, a person blames others. This is to pinpoint and solve a problem without admitting to being a part of that problem. In blaming others, we avoid acknowledging our own behavior and shame.

As difficulties in the family increase—verbal abuse, imagined illnesses, alcohol- or drug-related accidents, job losses—shame deepens. It becomes a dark, deep river running through the family. Help and answers are needed, and blame seems to provide them. Dad's drinking gets blamed on Mother's anger; Mom's anger gets blamed on her new job; and poor grades get blamed on the son's choice of friends. By blaming others, family members get to assign responsibility for the family's failure and shame. The person at fault, then, must resolve the problem that she supposedly created—others are relieved of this responsibility. Placing blame has the additional benefit of allowing family members, particularly children, to explain to themselves why they are different and don't fit in with other families. Judith tells how shame exiled her and her family from their community:

> My family was so ashamed of what we had become that we were afraid to be around normal families. Go to work and come home—that was life. Relatives would call and invite us to get together, and we always refused. The calls stopped coming. We didn't go anywhere. Our family vacation spot was a cabin twenty miles away from our home. The TV was our best friend, and most of us fell in love with the computer and the Internet. It gave us a chance to be with people without really having to be with people. Through the computer, the loneliness decreased for a time.

## How Much Can a Family Take?

Toward the end of stage 2, the family and its members show signs of severe deterioration. Members may experience imagined or very real health issues.

Humans can take only so much pain. Pain, whether it is physical or psychological, indicates that something is wrong. Attention needs to be paid; solutions need to be found. If a family doesn't find a way to end the pain, warning signs will only get louder.

In a 1990 study, the Children of Alcoholics Foundation found that children of alcoholics were admitted to hospitals 24.3 percent more than other children. Children of alcoholics also stayed 28.8 percent longer at hospitals.

As this study shows, everyone in an addicted family is susceptible to harm as a result of addictions. Jennifer remembers how upset her stomach got walking home from school each day:

> Every night as I walked home from school, I could feel my stomach starting to hurt. I was eating Tums left and right. Mom took me to the doctor a couple of times, and when they asked if I was under any stress, Mom looked at me so I said, "No, nothing more than the normal kid." How was I to tell her and the doctor that my brother would get high and torture me when they weren't around? I hoped they'd notice the cigarette burns on my feet, but they didn't. Instead, it was my stomach that had them worried. It wasn't until my brother got arrested for doing this to someone other than his sister that they asked if he had done these things to me. If he hadn't been in jail, I don't know if I would have told them. I was that scared of him. He wasn't just an addict—he was crazy, mean crazy.

# Summary of How the Addictive Process Affects the Family

## STAGE 2—DEVELOPMENT OF PROTECTIVE PERSONA

| | |
|---|---|
| **Effects on Communication:** | Dialogue is almost nonexistent; most communication is a monologue. |
| | Each family member develops a defensive persona to defend against increased emotional attacks and disappointments. |
| | Listening decreases and reactiveness increases. |
| | Everyone turns away from truths. |
| | Blame becomes a major defense mechanism. |
| **Effects on Family Interaction Patterns:** | The addict has emotionally separated from the family. |
| | The addict's primary relationship is now with the object of addiction. |
| | The co-addict's pursuit of the addict and attempts to control the addict increase. |
| | Family interaction becomes more and more organized around and affected by the addiction. |
| | Denial increases. |
| | A predator mentality develops as family members act more and more from their drives for power. |
| | The family begins operating from a system of shame. |

**Fig. 8**

*continued on next page*

| Emotional Effects on Family: | Feelings of anxiety, hurt, and sadness are regularly covered up by anger or denial. |
| --- | --- |
| | The family is internally experiencing grief over the loss of what it once had. |
| | Indifference and apathy become primary defenses. They increase in direct proportion to the degree of hurt being experienced. |
| | Crisis starts to function as a release of emotion. |

**Fig. 8**

## CHAPTER 5

# STAGE 3:
# HOPELESSNESS

After many years of living with addiction, a family exhausts its resources. Hopelessness sets in. Indifference becomes the primary coping mechanism of this last stage of family addiction. Deep, unfathomable sadness afflicts the family. Parents and children alike are tired; they can hardly manage their own lives.

Human beings have attachment needs. At this stage, most family members know that their needs will not be met through the family, except by forming *negative attachments*. In a negative attachment, one person's negative defense mechanisms play into those of another. For example, Mom distances herself from her own pain by putting down her husband in front of their children, and soon the youngest son joins in and mocks his own father. The mother and son become "partners." They are negatively attached whenever the son criticizes his father. A kind of camaraderie connects them. Negative attachments entangle everyone and reinforce negative defense systems. Family relationships become competitive and adversarial.

Living in this climate eventually becomes too much for any family. Members work to escape the family as soon as possible. Those who can set up lives outside of the family that offer a sense of fulfillment and purpose. For example, some find that joining the military provides hope and a new life away from the dysfunctional family. Cal recalls how it worked for him:

> I am so grateful that I was able to enlist in the marines early and that my parents didn't try to stop me. That was the best gift they ever gave me. I think they knew I was nearing my breaking point. I have a wonderful life in here. I'm a good soldier; after all, I've lived in a war zone all my life. At least here it's honest; we play "soldier" and I don't have to play "family" anymore. In the service, I know where the drunks are and I can stay away from them.

Cal is like many children in addictive homes who struggle to find alternatives to their families—service, marriage, out-of-town colleges. Some choices are positive, and some aren't. Some kids join gangs. All of them are seeking a new forum where they can gain a sense of purpose and belonging.

## Gulfs Seem Unbridgeable

The distance between family members grows in stage 3. Parents and siblings rarely connect with anyone sitting across from them at the kitchen table. For some members, this brings relief and comfort. Others experience deep shame, especially parents who may secretly long for their chemically dependent child to go away. Cindy was one such parent:

My son is a heroin addict and has had three or four detoxes and treatment. He has never been more than a year sober. All the other mothers tell "son stories" and get to brag, while I sit in silence and smile nicely at their stories. I feel so angry and pained inside. Even if my son did get sober, it may take years for me to get through my anger, hurt, and resentments. I've become bitter. I have a secret shame. I have at times found myself hoping he would die of an overdose. I hate myself for even having these thoughts. I believe I'm the worst mother on the face of the earth. Whenever I've had these thoughts, I get sick to my stomach and cry about the person I've become. I still remember holding him as a baby, staring into his big beautiful eyes, and telling him of my dreams for him. It hurts to remember those times—not because of how he has changed, but because of how I have changed.

The shame Cindy feels for wishing her son dead is common for parents of addicts. At this stage, it's not unusual for the addicts themselves to wish they were dead. These thoughts are coping mechanisms. When one feels hopeless, it's not abnormal to fantasize about suicide or the death of the person causing your pain. Most family members are too entangled to understand this, so they beat themselves up for entertaining these thoughts. This is especially true of parents. Years ago while working at a crisis invention center, I facilitated groups for parents of kids who were abusing drugs and alcohol. The parents experienced deep shame and anguish, believing their child's addiction was their fault. Many of them thought about their child dying and would berate themselves for allowing even one such thought to enter their minds. It got so some parents would refer to their "secret shame," and most of the members of the group knew what they were talking about.

This secret shame often leads parents to serious depression. Some parents compensate for their negative thoughts and busy themselves by helping their children. Jay's mother needed much help herself when he entered treatment:

> I didn't understand it until we were in treatment. Mom told me about how lost she got emotionally and how, at times, when at the end of her rope, she had thoughts of wishing I were dead. She told me her guilt caused her "busy times." I would come home and find my room totally clean, my shirts washed and ironed, with maybe a twenty-dollar bill in a pocket. I'd get my favorite meals for the next week or so. In treatment, I told my mom I understood. I couldn't stand myself and had thought of ending it all. I told her how proud I was of her. I asked her to forgive herself. It was the first time in years that both of us could look each other in the eyes and not be ashamed. Someday I'm going to surprise her and have her room totally clean and things ironed and have a twenty, well maybe a ten, hanging out of her pocket.

## Living in a State of Trauma

In this final stage of addiction, family members experience constant trauma, and people act as if danger is always nearby. A slammed door, a suddenly blaring radio, and loud voices startle everyone. Family members may spook easily. This may trigger more fights and quarreling. Kim displayed signs of the trauma she lived with daily:

I walked around that house on pins and needles. You never knew what might happen. I found myself starting to flinch at school when people made sudden quick moves. Loud noises would send a chill up my spine and my stomach would do somersaults. I know that all of this comes from living in this house with two addicts vying for who can kill themselves first. I am so sick of watching people hurt themselves! One and half more years and then I'm free. I'm already doing as much baby-sitting as possible to get money and leave the house. I learned to put my money in the bank, because once Dad found my hiding spot and spent two months of my baby-sitting earnings on one drunken weekend.

In this hopeless stage, exiting the family is a common strategy and solution. Kids often run away, enter the service or college, move into an apartment, get pregnant and marry, or join gangs. An addict's spouse may plan a divorce, divorce or separate, find a job that keeps her out of the house as much as possible, have an affair, or volunteer— anything to get out.

Anger may keep a few family members from total despair. Anger is their last hope, a buoy until they can exit the home. But for some, especially children, anger would be a dangerous strategy. These children use a different approach.

In their book *Traumatic Stress*, Bessel A. van der Kolk, Alexander C. McFarlane, and Lars Weisaeth discuss how some children will attach themselves to the sickest in a family through "traumatic bonding." By supporting or appearing to support the addict, children experience a connection that protects them or secures their relationships.

This is the "If you can't lick them, join them" approach. Traumatic bonding makes the individual, especially children, feel special and safe; however, they are actually bonding with someone who endangers them. Nick describes how this happened to him:

> It was my job to go to the bar and walk Dad home. Part of the ritual included me sitting on the barstool next to him and him sneaking me a beer. We had to sneak the beer because I was only ten, but drinking together bonded us. I was Dad's special kid. Special all right! Some nights I was scared to death I wouldn't have the strength to get him home, especially when he wanted to lean on me to avoid falling down. I would do push-ups at home to build up my arm strength. Boy, was I glad when I hit adolescence and started to grow and get stronger.

## Some Just Give Up

Those children and spouses who work to *get out* of the addictive household may experience less psychological damage than those who *give up*. A person who works to get out exhibits a hope for the future, a desire to find a place to reestablish oneself. Many in addictive families, however, give up. Seeing no way out, they submit blindly to the insanity of the addictive family system. Depression is their refuge. They are the ones who have given up interest, hope, or any dream of escape; they have also run out of anger. At this point, they're more vulnerable to addiction themselves. Stuart is a good example:

> I saw no reason to have emotions. They were nothing but a way for others to hurt you. I decided

to find a way not to have to feel anymore. Bingo! Smoke dope. All I had to do is take a hit or two and the circuits were shut down. They could fight, argue, and do whatever they wanted. If the noise got too loud, I'd just take another hit and tune them out. People had become pain. But with smoke, I could put up with people, and I even found a few I could like.

Stuart's actions were a version of "If you can't beat them, join them." By escaping into drug use himself, Stuart exited the family without even leaving the house.

## Connections No Longer Hold

As the addiction progresses, communication patterns become routine, stagnant, and rigid. Families repeat the same safe conversation or have none at all. If a family member drifts from the safe and predictable subjects, others bring the person back to safer ground. Children, sports, politics, weather, particular people, TV schedules, and speculation about what to do if the family wins the lottery are examples of safe subjects. These conversations offer an artificial sense of family. Deeper or more intimate conversations are avoided, as they're too emotionally laden and require a certain staying power that the addictive family in this stage doesn't have. Dwight and his alcoholic family demonstrate how communication deteriorates:

> Life was so boring at home, but we saw ourselves as close. It got to the point that, depending on what time it was, you'd know what conversations would be happening. If it was 5:30, we'd have the *What's for Supper* or *Can't We Have Something Different* chat. Supper was mainly quiet, and then at 7:00

we'd start the *What's on TV Tonight* discussion. No one dared talk about Dad sitting in the corner of the sofa getting hammered. Each week we'd watch the same shows, mainly so we could talk about the characters and their lives. These were our most exciting conversations. We read magazines to have bits of information to share about the lives of these people. Their lives helped us to avoid ours. I remember once my sister Carol brought up a serious personal issue, and all of us just turned and looked at her; we said nothing, just stared at her. She looked so embarrassed. We had basically shamed her for wanting to add something real into our lives.

If someone like Carol in the alcoholic family breaks the "no-talk" rule, there are consequences. Meaningful conversation is not allowed within the addicted family. If it does, it happens in subgroups or with people outside the family. Shame and embarrassment, however, keep family members from sharing too much with outsiders.

There are exceptions to these rules. During times of crisis, everyone gets the go-ahead to vent their feelings. However, after all is said, little is usually taken seriously, and nothing is resolved. Conversation again falls apart. The family believes issues are unsolvable. However, the family may turn to one person, like Lois, who has been assigned the role of hero or translator to make sense of what is fundamentally senseless:

Whenever there was a problem, I was to solve it. No one in the family believed that as a family we could solve anything—we could *fight* about anything, but I was seen as the solution-giver. At first

I saw this as an honor, then later as a burden. It continued even after I left home and had my own family. I would get calls from Mom and Dad about everything. Once they called because the phone company changed its name and my parents thought that meant they had to resubscribe for service. I know part of it was how lonely they were, but they had trained themselves—and I had helped—to be incompetent.

Heroes like Lois end up trapped. They find it hard to let others down and care for themselves, even after they have exited the family. One of the most troubling aspects of addiction for families is how lonely and isolated family members feel. Addiction becomes a cage wherein each family member is locked, and the keys or spiritual principles upon which the family life was once based are long lost.

## Need for New System

In this third and final stage of family addiction, the ability to connect and sustain relationships within the family has eroded significantly. Couples or parents cannot connect with each other long enough to solve problems. Though decisions get made, they rarely bring solutions. In this final stage, family relationships are primarily a source of pain and fear.

The addictive family now cycles in a hopeless mode or disintegrates unless the members seek an entirely new way of being with each other. Any system, however, including families, naturally resists change. In addictive families, a powerful force seems to work against change, even though everyone is miserable with the way things are. Change would force everyone to face the truth about themselves as individuals and as a unit. Change means something so alien to the addictive family members, they can't imagine what it might be. The idea of living in a different way increases their fear tenfold. The situation seems hopeless.

Next, we will discuss how the addictive process affects couples and children. Addicts, because of their isolation and self-centeredness, may believe that they are hurting no one but themselves—but this could not be further from the truth. In part 3, we'll look at how addiction affects the marital relationship and how it affects children growing up within an environment of addiction.

# Summary of How the
# Addictive Process Affects the Family

### STAGE 3—HOPELESSNESS

| | |
|---|---|
| **Effects on Communication:** | Dialogue is basically nonexistent. |
| | A "no-talk" rule takes effect—no real direct communication is allowed. |
| | Communication centers around "safe subjects" such as the school day, workday, or evening television schedule. |
| | Communication is often reduced to short, quick statements. |
| **Effects on Family Interaction Patterns:** | Addict is emotionally separated from family. |
| | Family rituals, routines, values, and beliefs that supported the family have been destroyed. |
| | Co-addicts stop pursuing the addict and give up on the relationship. |
| | The family works at *staying together* instead of *being together.* Separation and distance from the family are now effective strategies for keeping the family intact. |
| | Family interaction is more negative than positive. |
| | Negative attachments are the only form of connection between family members. |
| **Emotional Effects on Family:** | Family life creates much more pain than joy. |
| | The family is now seen and felt as an emotional burden by its members. Indifference and apathy are primary defense mechanisms. |
| | Depression among family members is common. Anger can become a way to fight depression. |
| | An environment of trauma is established. |

Fig. 9

# HOW THE ADDICTIVE PROCESS AFFECTS FAMILY RELATIONSHIPS

# Introduction to Part 3

## Scene 3

Ted Jensen sat staring at Maggie across the room, remembering the morning they had met at Hampton Junior College. It was the first day of their English class, and he sat in the auditorium two chairs down from her. He would come to love her passion and adventurous spirit. There wasn't anything she wouldn't try once, she had told him on one of their dates. She called herself the kite and him her string. Where had they gone wrong? Their wedding was just what each had hoped for. They had written their own vows. A few years later he was in the hospital room, standing alongside her, holding her hand when David was born. So they couldn't have another child; it wasn't anyone's fault—or was it? Was this the reason she drank so much and got so mean? Was she blaming herself? She never blamed him, except when she was drunk. He hated it when she drank.

Over the years, the good times became fewer and fewer. God, he wanted his old Maggie back. He had begged and fought to keep her happy and away from the bottle, but nothing worked. Where had they gone wrong? This question kept haunting him, along with all the cruel things he and Maggie had said to each other when she drank.

Maggie sat in the living room on the couch opposite him. She seemed to get that dark mood about her, Ted thought. It actually seemed to change the color of her *complexion. Maggie watched television and never noticed him looking at her. He wondered where they—once dreaming of a future, happy to be with each other—had now disappeared. She was no longer enthusiastic, but adrift in the sky; he no longer felt that she was attached to him, David, or anyone. Could they ever reconnect?*

## Family Relationships Meet Addiction

Much like a riverbed, a psychological channel of intimacy forms between couples in marriages and partnerships. Normally, we work to keep these channels open, flowing, and ever-widening, but when addiction floods these channels, they become clogged and polluted with frustration, resentment, despair, and fear. Relationships become extremely difficult. Eventually, these channels shut down and relationships fall apart. Addiction destroys intimacy and love, and for this reason, family relationships will always take the brunt of the addictive process. In this section, we'll look more closely at the destructive effects of addiction on couples and children.

# CHAPTER 6

# COUPLES
## AND THE
# ADDICTIVE
# PROCESS

## Becoming a Couple

People become attracted to each other for countless reasons. It might be chemistry, common interests, or physical attraction. Couples themselves can't always explain why or even how they fell in love. The reasons why two people eventually go beyond dating to commit themselves in marriage or partnership are many. Some couples may view marriage as a ritual or formal announcement of their love for each other. Some couples may naively believe that marriage offers them never-ending happiness. Others might use marriage to escape bad situations at home. Still others might seek security and support in a loving partnership. Perhaps an unplanned pregnancy or the hope of creating a family brings two people together. Or a couple may bond out of a fear of being alone. Whatever the reason, all couples hope to create and sustain love between the partners. How likely or unlikely this hope may be is beside the point. Everyone seeks love and fulfillment, not destruction, from relationships.

Individuals can find meaning and fulfillment from a variety of activities besides marriage, such as working, creating art, or even accepting physical challenges. A marriage or partnership with another, however, is undoubtedly one of the most profound ways to create meaning. Existentialist and Holocaust survivor Viktor Frankl states in his book *Man's Search for Meaning* that one of the three ways to find meaning in life is to truly love and experience another.* In love, we allow ourselves to be profoundly changed by the other. The process of becoming a "meaningful couple" is similar to the process of creating meaning for any individual (see part 1).

Marriage or partnership creates an arena in which we can define, explore, refine, and defend our principles of betterment that contribute to a meaningful existence. A "successful" marriage or union results when two people can

---

*Viktor E. Frankl describes three ways to create meaning: (1) by doing a deed; (2) by experiencing a value (here he explains that one way to experience a value is by experiencing someone through love); and (3) by taking a new attitude toward unavoidable suffering. Herein lies the dilemma that the co-addict faces. This person is finding meaning through experiencing another, and all of a sudden, the addictive process takes that person away. The co-addict is forced to find meaning in a new way. The only way for the co-addict to find meaning now must be from Frankl's third way—in the attitude she takes toward the unavoidable suffering being experienced. This is why Al-Anon can be so helpful. In Al-Anon, the co-addict can focus on herself and, through the principles of recovery, discover a new way to acquire meaning and love in life.

*together* create and sustain meaning and love within their relationship.

Created love—the higher and more developed form of love—always contains a paradox. Every couple's love is in essence a mathematical mystery in which one and one must somehow add up to three. Independence and mutuality, two seemingly opposing principles, must coexist to create a third: love. Both individuals must remain firm in their identity and must give up enough of themselves and their egos to create a *we*. The partners remain individuals and sacrifice themselves for the good of the relationship.

In order for two people to become a true couple, based on trust and comfort, each must sacrifice ego at the appropriate times and in appropriate ways during the development of their relationship. At first, the two people are only *acting* as a couple. It's only after surrendering and sacrificing ego a number of times that they cross an invisible line and are transformed. Then, they begin being a couple. Being a couple means preserving and nurturing the *we*. How a couple will balance independence and mutuality in their relationship is critical to their survival and prosperity.

If neither or only one is willing to sacrifice ego, the *we* of the couple can never develop enough to withstand the pressures of life. Without the *we*, couples never develop a heart or soul to their relationship. Their relationship will end, or the couple will stay together knowing, openly or secretly, that there is no real bond between them. One client, Bonnie, recalled the day she realized that she alone was working on her marriage. "I gave and gave," she said. "I kept doing what I thought you had to do to make a relationship work. The more I gave, the less my husband seemed to give. After a while I got scared and felt alone and at times stupid. I was haunted by the question, Am I the only one who cares if this thing works?"

Why wouldn't an individual sacrifice enough ego to allow the *we* to develop? There are many reasons besides addiction, but addiction is one of the strongest and most painful reasons. Although an addicted person may truly desire intimacy, to create a *we*, the illness of addiction prevents it. The addict simply is not able to create and sustain a meaningful, loving relationship; he no longer possesses the tools to create intimacy.

As a result, the chemically dependent family experiences immense frustration and pain. Mutuality, or the bond between the couple in a healthy relationship, is what the addictive process attacks and destroys. In every fiber of their bodies, a couple will know they have failed. The only difference between the husband and wife, the addicted and co-addict, is how each will deal with this pain and despair. Most often, the addict takes the pain deeper into the addictive process. Drinking and drugging are quick fixes. The co-addict partner experiences the loss differently because this person finds no comfort or reprieve from a bottle or drug. However, the co-addict may chase his partner into the muck of the addictive process. Although the co-addict is only trying to rescue the addict from a life mired in self-centeredness and loneliness, his actions actually mire himself in loneliness.

## The Shift

Earlier we discussed how couples come together. If a couple continue dating, exploring each other's beliefs and values, they will eventually shift from thinking of themselves as individuals to thinking of themselves as a couple. Rarely can anyone identify exactly when or where this happens.

But when this shift occurs, a desire to formalize the relationship develops. A decision or pronouncement will follow sooner or later. This decision is often made public. A couple may decide to marry and stand before a judge or minister, family, friends, or God and vow they will love each other "forever." Or the decision may be kept private, as with unmarried couples who live together year after year but are no less committed or "married."

Getting married or moving in together attempts to resolve some of the questions we all must answer: Is it better to go through life with a partner? Do I trade my *me* in for a *we*? In order for two people to become a meaningful and loving couple, they must answer yes to these questions. The belief that life can be better together than alone is critical and fundamental to every relationship. Without it, true attachment cannot occur. This belief will comfort a couple when they find ways to honor it and haunt them when they do not.

## A Couple's Agreement: The *Why* of Being a Couple

When two people decide to become a couple, they agree to certain things. The agreements may be spoken or unspoken. Like a contract based on a couple's hopes, dreams, and desires for a better life together, these initial agreements help define the couple's shared principles and values. The agreements try to answer questions such as, "What are we about? What kind of relationship are we forming? Will we be monogamous? Will we support each other's career? How can we fight more fairly?" The agreements are meant to direct the relationship's course. They will become standards by which the couple will judge the success or failure of the relationship.

Because the beginning of most relationships, before agreements are formalized, is a time of giving, respecting, and watching out for the other, most couples start out with good basic agreements. The agreements are usually about love and meaning, not about power and pleasure. In time, as couples begin to articulate their agreements and hopes, they are defining not only *how* but also *why* they want to be together. The why of every relationship is critical to its existence and development. The agreements help clarify why the partners love each other and want a life together. The couple's agreements may be *formal, informal,* or *assumed.*

The *formal* aspect of agreements includes those statements, ideas, and plans that each partner makes with the other. They are the covenants a couple make together publicly or privately. We've heard these formal pronouncements, or vows, at weddings. A couple agree to love each other forever and do whatever is needed for the marriage to work. The formality of the agreement rests in the declarations they consciously make to each other.

*Informal* agreements are made after knowing a person over a period of time. They involve conscious and deliberate decisions to help your partner grow and have a good life. After years, a person comes to know the other's hopes and dreams. For example, a wife finally realizes her husband regrets not finishing his college degree and wishes to do so. Or a husband may realize that his wife has always wanted to visit Spain or France. These dreams are usually not articulated directly but rather are expressed through everyday conversation. A person's dreams, hopes, and desires aren't always proclaimed in a formal fashion, as in vows or contracts, but they are a part of every relationship. For instance, your partner's parents might be very important to her, so you work to be the best in-law you can be, because you have informally agreed to fulfill your partner's dreams and wishes.

*Assumptions* often remain unconscious unless they are threatened. Although assumptions are rarely verbalized, they are basic to every relationship. For instance, we assume that we'll be physically safe in our relationships and our partners won't steal from us or injure us. We often assume our partners will wear their wedding rings when traveling. We would be shocked to find our assumptions wrong. We assume that our partners like us and will not engage in criminal behavior. We believe, even if it's not declared in a formal way, that our partners will treat us with respect and dignity. When these basic assumptions prove to be wrong, we feel the core of the relationship attacked. Tracy, whose husband was an addictive gambler, was in shock when she discovered how wrong she was about her assumed agreements with her husband. Her husband had stolen her jewelry. "I never in my wildest fantasy thought my husband would steal from me," she said. "Then one day I found out he had taken my jewelry— the jewelry my grandmother had left me—and sold it. How was I to know this would happen?" She couldn't. It's natural to assume that our partners will not steal from us.

These formal, informal, and assumed agreements are based on *mutual vulnerability* Healthy relationships have an unselfish quality about them. Embedded within a couple's agreement are fundamental principles that the partners are staking their relationship and happiness on. The agreements express the couple's belief that each will do and sacrifice what is needed to create and sustain a meaningful *we*.

After a couple have made formal and informal agreements and assumptions, each person is responsible for following through. This often means learning how to put the agreements ahead of individual desires and working to keep the agreements. Normally, ego struggles will occur while the couple try to integrate the agreements into daily life. Behavior changes will be necessary. Life may test and challenge the agreements. This is normal. Changes to their agreements will have to be negotiated.

At this stage, the most important choices concern *how* the couple will solve struggles. Though the partners now have agreements, they still may interpret the agreements differently. *How* a couple solve differences or argue is more important than *what* they argue about. A couple may disagree over what to spend their money on. One may feel a new microwave is more important for the family than a new television. The issue may be settled when one partner uses anger and intimidation to get what she wants. The partner's behavior, however, violates the couple's formal agreement to respect each other. The struggle produces distance, resentments, and mistrust.

*Every couple will use either power, pleasure, or meaning to solve differences.* To create and sustain a deep, abiding love, the couple must regularly choose the drive for meaning— the principles of betterment—over power and pleasure. *Remember, love is a by-product of putting principles of betterment into action.* Only then do love and meaning become teachers of and friends to power and pleasure.

For every couple, time eventually becomes a friend or a foe. The better partners do over time at honoring their commitment, bringing meaning to their lives, and making necessary changes to their agreements, the happier and more competent each will feel as an individual and as part of a couple. As years pass, they feel more trusting and grateful for their relationship. Time then becomes an ally for the couple, as principles of betterment are continually brought to the relationship and put into action. These principles become spiritual habits that lead a couple back to meaning and their agreements when they get lost. All couples will at times lose sight of their agreements and principles; however, these principles become a lantern so they can find their way in the darkest of times.

When couples fail to use meaning, or principles of betterment, to create and sustain their relationship, time becomes an archenemy and foe. If couples aren't able to fulfill their agreements, if they betray what they had agreed to work for, each partner experiences discomfort as a couple and as an individual. This discomfort can quickly become despair. Then, the relationship may break down into power struggles. Couples then feel more intensely the lack of meaning in their exchanges, which weighs on them individually and as a couple. Often this pressure becomes too much. *Who* is wrong becomes more important than *what* is wrong. As each month goes by, things only seem to worsen. They may feel intense pressure to change. The most common mistake couples make is to try to solve their struggles with either power or pleasure.

If the drive for pleasure becomes a couple's primary orientation, both individuals try to avoid the pain that is naturally a part of being a couple. A pleasure-driven couple will try to resolve the problem by avoiding it. However, avoidance only brings more pain. Each partner may seek other forms of pleasure. Some may return to old friendships or create new ones, not to benefit the relationship but to avoid the emptiness they feel within their relationship. One or both may seek pleasure from some other person, object, or event. Betrayal may happen. At this time, many are seduced into the addictive process. A client, Mark, spoke about how drinking helped him avoid his responsibilities:

> When I realized my relationship wasn't working out, I started to drink heavier and more regularly. I knew it wasn't right, but I was in so much pain, felt so lost, that I needed relief. When we had married, we promised each other companionship and pleasure, and now we couldn't spend an evening together without bringing pain to each other. Alcohol became my way to numb this out.

If a couple's primary orientation becomes power, both partners will try to force their own version of the initial agreements. This sets up a dominant-submissive relationship or a stalemate if the power is divided up equally. Each person feels right and fights for his or her opinion or point of view. Both partners quickly become self-righteous. Any empowerment they experience stems not from working well together, but from getting their own way. Their power (and pleasure) comes from winning. Yet this kind of fight produces no real winners. When partners battle over who is right and who is wrong, both lose. The couple become more distant and experience increasing isolation and pain. Although egos may be satisfied by skillfully belittling or defeating the other, the "victory" comes at the cost of the relationship. Linda, a forty-year-old wife and recovering alcoholic, elaborates on the nature of this problem:

> I got everything I wanted. I won all our disagreements. If I believed I was right, I would fight until I won. But truthfully there were times, many times, I knew I was wrong or I didn't know what the truth was. I pretended I did. I became powerful in an

empty way. I'd get into bed at night and feel the coldness that seemed to wedge itself between us. My blanket of self-righteousness was all that kept me warm. I pulled it tight around me and fell asleep hoping that the next day would be better.

All couples experience difficult times in working through struggles. It isn't unusual for struggles to become based on power or pleasure. Ideally, each partner will realize the futility of such arguments and discover or return to more meaningful ways to solve issues. In most relationships, if not all, the partners need to work and rework their initial agreements into deeper, more meaningful agreements that both are able to live by.

## When Addiction Enters a Relationship

Earlier, we saw that every couple in an enduring relationship must eventually decide that being together serves them better than being apart. Addiction, however, opposes the very notion of togetherness. It increases personal isolation, creates dividing conflicts, enhances egotism, and destroys intimacy. Addiction runs counter to the essence and purpose of being a couple.

When addiction enters a relationship, a couple's formal and informal agreements covertly change. Even their assumptions are tested by this powerful illness. Addiction can be more powerful than any couple's agreement. It depletes the strengths of the relationship. The alcoholic or drug addict abandons her primary relationship with a human being for a primary relationship with an object (drug) and an event (a bar's happy hour).

As the addiction progresses, the chemically dependent

person detaches from being a couple. Her ego—that is, *me*—becomes more important than the *we*. Soon the addict unconsciously returns to a life where she is going it alone. However, the addict suffers from the illusion that she still has a "good" relationship. Though the addict is emotionally more attached and committed to the addictive process than to the other person, she may insist to her spouse that they're still in love, a couple, a *we*.

The co-addict is not convinced; he senses how the addict is living less like a couple and more like a separate individual. This frightens the co-addict. The essence of the agreement has been changed, and he wasn't even consulted. At first, the addict's shift in priorities shows up in small breaks in the couple's agreements. Maybe the addict stops calling to let her partner know she will be late; the addict may make up stories that seem a little suspicious. Her tone may sound disrespectful. Maybe the addict shuts off dialogue in conversation and becomes self-righteous after a few drinks. There are countless ways the addict or alcoholic can dishonor the couple's initial agreement. The chemically dependent person finally tears herself from the *we* of the couple, creating deep pain and loss within this relationship.

The breakdown of the couple's initial agreement creates anxiety in the relationship. The addict reacts by falling further under the spell of the addiction process. She drinks more, stays out later, suffers more consequences from her behavior. The addict's denial also increases; she believes nothing is different. Addicts will get more defensive and argumentative, especially when something threatens their illusion of normalcy. They feel more shameful and make promises to do better in the future, but these promises are short-lived. As addicts move further into the addictive process, they betray their relationships—and themselves—more and more. Agreements break down further, causing more anxiety.

In addiction, the addicted person is involved in an internal fight with himself. On a preconscious level, he can sense that he's fighting for his life. However, he's also in an external fight with the person he loves, who wants him to stop using drugs or alcohol. The addict, unlike his partner, sees the substance of abuse as the problem *and* the solution. Anxiety increases, and the addict runs further into the addiction.

Because the co-addict finds no refuge in drinking or addiction, she seeks more power and control to reduce her anxiety. This person expends an enormous amount of energy trying to keep the alcoholic sober, mend fences the addict has broken, and make phone calls to work reminding the addicted person to come straight home after picking up groceries. The partner desperately wants a return to what was.

The co-addict really wants his friend, lover, and partner back; he longs for the love that was protected and provided for by their initial agreements. This is why co-addicts often seem to be chasing after their addicted partners. They want their partners back. But the addict only runs faster and farther into her addiction, which in turn makes the co-addict partner more frantic and desperate. This is not abnormal, sick, or dysfunctional. This is normal. This is the essence of love. People naturally panic when their love is threatened. Out of love or hope, the co-addict continues to make profound personal sacrifices for the sake of the relationship and the other person, the addict. The sacrifices, however, aren't healing the relationship as they might in a normal situation, but are actually harming it further. When a person makes genuine sacrifices for a deteriorating relationship and when these sacrifices are ridiculed, the co-addict feels more humiliation and anger, and a desire to distance himself from the source of the pain—the addict.

The co-addict is in a relationship with someone who may truly love him, but who is unable to adequately demonstrate this love. In essence, the addict's love has become meaningless. The partner of the addict can sense the love but never experience it in a meaningful way. A horrible situation! The co-addict is starving and must walk daily past a bakery with no door.

Co-addicts react by becoming keeper of the couple's agreements. They remember every word and promise the partners made to each other. They may ask: "Why do you treat me and yourself like this? Don't you love me anymore? Why are you acting as if you don't care? I know you do! Why are you so disrespectful to me? Why don't you treat me like you used to? Will you promise never to act like this again?" Embedded in each of these questions are the couple's broken agreements. Remember, the co-addict partner is desperate to restore the couple's agreements, restore meaning, and rebuild the *we* of the relationship. Co-addicts believe in what they're fighting for. As they feel betrayed and beaten up by the addiction itself, the rightness of their "mission" becomes the salve on their wounds. Over time they face the very real danger of becoming self-righteous.

Time is now a foe of the couple and a friend to the addictive process. The longer it takes for the addict or alcoholic to get help, the further the relationship deteriorates. Because of real and ever-present dangers in the addictive process, each day brings intense anxiety. Car accidents, missed work, injuries at home, other illnesses, and even delirium tremens (d.t.'s) threaten the couple. Every day is a struggle with addiction, and the couple lives further and further from the essence of their initial agreement. Love no longer seems to promise a better life. Their courting days and promises become a kind of backdrop by which they judge their failures. Pain deepens, and once again anxiety increases. The couple's history has become a burden instead of a comfort.

At some point co-addicted partners become so frustrated, lost, and beaten up by the addictive process that they secretly give up on meaning and love. They come to desire power. They believe power over the other can protect them. Once they knew they were the keepers of meaning and love, but now they don't believe in themselves. This becomes their secret shame. Half the time they aren't even aware of their own fatalism. They deny to themselves they have given up on love. Katrina recounts her despair in an alcoholic marriage:

> I just couldn't take it anymore. The drinking, the lying, the problems, everything. I was sick of it. I, the one who had hopes and dreams, the one who had pushed for this marriage, now secretly wished he would die, just so the suffering would be over. I was so ashamed. I begged him to act right "for the marriage," but I wanted out of the marriage. I was so ashamed, I couldn't tell anyone, especially my family and friends who had raised doubts.

Katrina, like many spouses married to alcoholics, secretly wanted to end the marriage. To admit this made her feel ashamed. At this point, the addictive process swallows up the co-addict, who has been beaten down to the point of complete despair. If someone puts a gun to your head, you don't try to initiate a meaningful conversation. You quietly submit. But once the person and the gun are gone, you most likely turn to friends and loved ones to help process and bring meaning and healing to the experience. Addiction puts a gun to the couple's head. It's understandable that spouses finally submit, despair, and quit. The addictive process overpowers a couple, disabling either partner to create and sustain a meaningful connection.

The co-addict's desire for power is natural and reasonable. The mistake lies in seeking raw power, not ethical power. At this point, the co-addict gets truly caught up and lost in the addictive process. She already feels shame for giving up on meaning and love.

The addict has long ago forsaken meaning for the power and pleasure found in the intoxication experience. But why exactly does the co-addict give up on meaning? There are many reasons. First, after repeatedly trying and failing to fix the relationship, this person feels powerless and frustrated, which in turn creates a natural desire for more power. Second, the addictive process regularly lays to waste the couple's hopes and dreams. When someone repeatedly puts a gun to your head, you naturally desire your own gun. Third, all of the co-addict's attempts to reconnect in meaningful ways with her loved one fail. Over time, the co-addict can make a good case to herself and others why meaning and love don't work. Finally, the co-addict is constantly drawn into power struggles with the addict. She naturally develops more defense mechanisms and toughens up. Remember, "An abnormal reaction to an abnormal situation is normal." If we keep Viktor Frankl's phrase in mind, we can see how normal the nonaddict's reaction really is. One can live under these conditions for only so long before giving up. When we feel powerless, it's normal to reach for power, though it's really a time to develop stronger skills that will help us keep meaning and love in our lives.

Though the struggle described here runs counter to the couple's initial agreement for a better life together, it isn't counter to the addictive process, which works to destroy meaningful relationships. Addiction is progressive. Inevitably, the addictive couple finally seek pleasure or power more than meaning. No matter what they do, both partners will feel ashamed, powerless, and afraid. The reason for this is simple: Whenever pleasure or power becomes the primary organizing principle, fear and shame naturally occur.

The pain the addicted couple feel is twofold. First, the partners are being separated from their love for each other. Second, as each replaces meaning with pleasure or power, they are being separated from the best of themselves and their own humanity. Each becomes someone the other finds hard to respect. They feel a growing distance between their hearts and heads, between their values and behaviors, during a time when the distance should be shortening.

The couple's agreement has changed from one of betterment to one of survival. Now they're struggling to stay together instead of struggling to be together. They ask themselves why they are in the relationship. Each becomes distant from the other and from herself or himself. They feel crazy inside, and this insanity is real. For as Fromm says in *The Art of Loving*: "The deepest need of man is the need to overcome his separateness to leave the prison of his aloneness. The absolute failure to achieve this aim means insanity."

It's impossible to be prepared for what is needed to protect and honor a relationship in the presence of addiction.

It's like trying to protect a side of beef from a hungry pack of wolves. One needs the very best and most advanced skills. This is what Alcoholics Anonymous and Al-Anon are about. These recovery programs teach needed skills by giving an individual a place to learn and be heard without being put down, attacked, or ridiculed. They reaffirm that love is good and needed and a meaningful experience. They can also show how addiction is an illness and how a couple's love alone cannot cure it.

Members of these recovery programs read, talk with others who have had similar experiences, and study the spiritual principles found within the Twelve Steps. Individuals are encouraged to understand how they, not their partners, have betrayed these principles. We are encouraged to see what we did wrong, not what others did. Taking our own inventories helps us define our own behavior and motivation. Members are supported in taking a long and hard look at how addiction has changed them.

Over time, couples can reconnect with what will heal them. They reconnect with a *we*, though at first the *we* may be the AA or Al-Anon group. They learn or relearn how to turn their will and lives over to the care of the group or Higher Power. They strategize how best to honor love, not how best to fix their partners. These are tough lessons. Some may learn they can't have what they desperately want. It's hard to hear you may not be able to save that which you love most: a relationship.

# Summary of How the Addictive Process Affects a Couple

1. The initial agreement about the *why* of the relationship breaks down.

2. Anxiety is created due to this breakdown.

3. Each person deals with anxiety in different ways, which only creates more anxiety.

4. The addicted partner treats the co-addict as an object and not as a person.

5. The relationship changes from being three-dimensional to being one-dimensional.

6. Relationship issues now get settled through manipulation instead of negotiation.

7. The communication changes from a dialogue to a monologue. Each person listens not for content but for ways to attack what the other is saying.

8. The co-addict becomes keeper of the initial agreement, but at some time will secretly give up on the agreement.

9. Time now works against the couple.

Fig. 10

# CHAPTER 7

# CHILDREN
## AND THE
# ADDICTIVE
# PROCESS

## A Child's Loss of Innocence and Meaningful Attachments

When it comes to growing up in an addictive system, few truths are carved in stone. It's difficult to make broad generalizations about the effects of growing up in an addictive family. However, two things are always true: (1) the addiction will affect every family member differently; and (2) although the addictive process will affect everyone, not everyone may be damaged by it. Addiction severely harms many children, yet others may find a way to leave these families as fairly developed and complete individuals. We call them *resilient children*.

For psychological health and growth, children need certain levels of protection, attachment, and guidance.

Childhood should be a time to explore, play, discover, question, sort out, and learn how to live a good life. Children will naturally get into mischief and learn how to get out of it. They need to be surrounded and raised in a meaningful and wholesome environment.

Unfortunately, children of addicts must live within what is most meaningless—addiction. For many of these children, childhood is often dangerous and senseless. Instead of enjoying their time of vulnerability, children of addicts work hard just to emotionally survive.

Family attachments, the powerlessness of the addictive system, and the child's vulnerability in the family become burdens to be shed as soon as possible. Though most children resent the limitations of their childhood, children of addicts see their limitations and powerlessness as the primary cause of their pain. They may develop intense fear and hatred of their own size and youth, which often causes them to dream of becoming big and powerful. They feel and sense that being a child holds danger.

Unable to understand how the addictive process is creating their pain, they blame themselves. "If only I were smarter…. If only I were big…. If only I were grown up." Each "if" is actually a silent condemnation of themselves and their youth. For these children, being smart, big, and tough will never end their pain of growing up in an alcoholic family. Children of addicts, like Ellen in the following story, never feel that they are big or smart enough:

> As a small child, I repeatedly dreamed of being big. It felt wonderful. In my mind I could become as tall or wide as the biggest building. I was Alice and I had stepped through the looking glass. It wasn't till I was older that I realized it was my drunken father

that I wanted to be more powerful and bigger than. As I got older, I craved power and I got it. Very few would go toe-to-toe with me in the business world. I kept fighting and winning, but this power could not cover up the emptiness I felt. Truthfully, I never really wanted to fight and conquer my father; I just wanted to love and be loved by him If the truth be known, I want to be small—small enough to be held and told that I'm good enough and that I can rest now. I don't know if this will ever happen because even in my personal relationships, I can't let go. I guess I'm still holding out for my dad, even though his alcoholism killed him and maybe my spirit years ago.

We must remember that children of addicts or alcoholics are children. They hold only the power of a child. This means they are trapped in a horrible situation without the power to change it. They're powerless over addiction, and their lives have become unmanageable. In the end, they lose two important aspects of childhood: *innocence* and *meaningful attachments*.

### Innocence

We are all born in a state of innocence. At birth, our hearts are genuine and our minds are active. We are born without knowledge of the ways of the world, without knowledge of evil and without the capacity to harm, injure, or corrupt others. Still, as precious as innocence is, we are as children ready to begin exchanging it for knowledge of the world. We desire knowledge.

The main job of parents is to protect their children from the people of the world who would steal their innocence and use it for their own purpose. Caregivers and parents must help their children feel comfortable within innocence and not be ashamed of it. Parents are not to threaten a child's innocence, but be guardians of it.

No one can remain in a state of innocence. We must go out into the world, learn its ways, and let it alter us. We become part of the world and learn things we perhaps had never wished or needed to learn. To be spiritual, we must also be worldly. In everyday life, we learn about the drives for pleasure, power, and meaning. We learn of our own ability to be kind, loving, and beautiful and our ability to be mean, hateful, and ugly. We also learn that others are capable of harming us and that we, too, are capable of harming others.

Only when we can see that we have both good and bad inside us can we choose to direct and dedicate our spirits in meaningful ways. Once we understand that we are body and soul, world and spirit, we can start to solve the paradox of how to honor both, but this involves pain. In this struggle, we must choose between meaning and power or pleasure. If we choose anything other than meaning for our lives, we will lose our way on the spiritual path. We'll find shortcuts, "easier, softer ways." Most who prefer the shortcut that pleasure and power seem to offer do so for three reasons: (1) fear of choosing; (2) denial that they have to make a choice; and (3) illusion that they have already made a choice. Addicts will always take the "softer way."

As we mature, we interact with the world and begin trading our innocence for knowledge. It's important to remember that our innocence is ours to trade when, where, and how we want. The more confident we feel about this exchange between ourselves and the world, the more trusting and safe we feel. Abuse occurs when one steals another's innocence for one's own ego gratification. It takes away a person's right to choose when and how to exchange innocence for knowledge.

There are two types of abuse: unintentional and intentional. To deprive children their choice to trade innocence for knowledge is cruel and causes pain, even when done unintentionally, as it happens with addiction. To do so intentionally is evil. It leaves children feeling unsafe and untrusting. It takes from them their fundamental right to innocence, as described by one of my clients:

> There is nothing wrong with sex, but for God's sake, I was only ten and I was given no choice. My innocence was mine to give, not his to take. I will always hate that thief.

Maturing involves going out into the world and trading innocence for knowledge, inexperience for experience, ignorance for wisdom. When children first attend school, they trade in their naiveté for responsibility, false or uninformed beliefs for accurate ones based on details and information. As we age, we experience and learn to accept the beauty and the ugliness of the world. The ugliness of the world will shape us just as strongly as the beauty. When we grow up, we leave our innocence—our wonderful but one-dimensional state—for a state that integrates the good and the bad, innocence and experience, truth and lies.

In making these "trades," we become worldly. Yet at some time, we must journey back to God's loving grace with our innocence restored and deepened. We can regain innocence by embracing love and developing a life based on spiritual discipline. We regain innocence by choosing to follow spiritual principles that foster, create, and sustain love. Spiritual discipline that is sustained develops into wise innocence or what is called *created innocence*—a mix of innocence and knowledge that is created when a person consistently chooses meaning and love over ugliness and hate. The sadness and the longing that children of addicts feel are partially a longing for innocence lost. Children of addicts live in a world where innocence is not honored and respected. All children unconsciously long for guidance in how to best manage and negotiate the trade of their innocence for knowledge. They long for meaningful parenting. Growing up in an addictive household that uses manipulation not negotiation puts children at a great disadvantage. They will learn skills not helpful to them, which could lead them to other manipulative people. Simply put, the language spoken at home is often the language we're drawn to. A client named Ed raises some important questions:

> Is it any wonder that I ended up running with the wrong crowd—hell, I was *raised* by the wrong crowd. My father was a drug dealer and my mother an alcoholic. By the time I was seven, I knew how to spot a deal going down and how to be on the lookout for the police. My first real parent was my counselor—whom I had a hard time trusting because he was kind to me. Isn't that crazy? My "second parent," whom I still see as my real parent, is my sponsor. He and my NA group became the right crowd for me. It feels good to have people around me who truly don't want me to get in trouble.

Exchanging innocence for knowledge needs to happen with as much dignity as possible and at developmentally correct times. If innocence is taken from us too early in life, we're forced to grieve. We feel a wound, an emptiness where our innocence was. Although we received knowledge, it lacks the ingredients of dignity, caring, and timeliness and so won't heal the wound. When we speak of "children who have grown up too fast," we're referring to children who have had to give up their innocence too soon.

Children whose innocence is taken too early react in many ways:

1. They build up defenses to try and wall off their feelings of loss and often become hard.

2. They seek pleasure sensations to fill up or cover up their loss.

3. They pretend that their innocence hasn't been lost and develop what Rollo May, in *Power and Innocence*, calls pseudo-innocence.

4. They pretend that meaning and love are not important to them.

5. They seek out people who promise to fill up their wounds.

6. They develop a fear of attaching to that which has meaning, because meaning may hook their shame and make them aware of their wounds.

### Attachment

Attachment, our drive for connection, is a basic need. It is a biological tool we're born with. John Bowlby, in his book *A Secure Base*, argues that an infant is born with an internal goal for attachment and will strive to meet this goal. The infant is born ready to bond. Thus, the family we're born into is exceedingly important. It's here we form our first and most lasting attachments.

As a newborn child bonds with family members, he starts the innocence-for-knowledge exchange process. The child is brought into the belief systems and lifestyle of his parents. Children attach not just to individuals, but also to a set of ideas, concepts, and principles. The child takes on his parents' assets and liabilities as his own.

Through repeated interactions with their parents, children construct mental models of their parents, themselves, and the world around them. These models help them appraise new situations and guide their behavior. As children develop and go out into the world, they will seek, develop, and create external social systems that support these internal social models. The more efficient, caring, secure, and functional are the child's interactions with his parents, the better the child's models and skills.

Children live in situations of forced attachment. This means they have no choice over who their parents are—they must attach to their parents for survival. Ideally, parents teach the children to attach also out of meaning and love.

Growing up involves learning to attach and stay attached to what is truly meaningful in life. This means we stick not only with the winners, but also with winning concepts, ideas, and principles. We develop self-esteem from attaching to that which can create and sustain meaning. Self-esteem is not something you are born with, but something you and others create. The better your attaching skills, the more self-esteem you'll have.

### Attachment Means Letting Go

Paradoxically, attachment involves letting go. To attach to something means we must let go of other things. When we make choices and attach to these choices, we're also saying no to other choices. When I said yes and married my wife, I was also saying no to other women.

The children of addicts are taught to connect to that

which is not useful in life and to let go of that which has greater value. They attach to an addictive family process instead of a healthy one. This is the major way that the addictive process hurts children throughout their lives. Children repeatedly see the addict or addicts, if both parents are chemically dependent, let go of important ideas, people, and principles and replace them with ideas, people, and principles that have little importance and are void of love. They are unfortunately experiencing the addictive process, not healthy parenting. Children would prefer to turn away from the addictive process but can't because they feel they would be turning away from their parents. Jane put it this way:

> My father was a good man, with good friends, work habits, ideas, and values. He was a man to be admired. *Dignity* and *respect* were words people used to describe him. But as his addiction progressed, good friends were replaced with bad ones, good work habits with bad work habits, respect for disgrace. Soon, he lost everything. But what I think killed him was his loss of dignity. He had been a lawyer. He loved law. Near the end of his life, he was arrested for shoplifting a bottle of wine. He never recovered. His addiction finally had him betray that which was most precious to him—justice.

Children of addicts, like most other children, love their parents. As they get older, however, they may want to let go of their parents yet feel guilty in doing this, especially if the timing is unnatural. So most children don't or can't entirely let go. When children of addicts crave parenting, as we all do from time to time, they may search for a friend and find someone who can't be a friend, a relationship that will go nowhere, or maybe a drug that will injure them. In doing so, they end up re-creating a familiar pattern of relationships that leave them more empty than fulfilled.

The desire to have a loving parent is so strong that even if the relationship with their parents is meaningless, children often add meaning that is not there. If their parents aren't acting like parents, the children may pretend otherwise. Many times during my years as an addictions counselor, I've listened to clients tell me how they know that the abuse and crazy behaviors they experienced as children were really acts of love. An extreme example of this was a man who talked of being branded with a hot poker by his abusive alcoholic father (he had the mark to prove it). This man was convinced his father did this so he would never forget him and the "lessons" he wanted him to learn.

The age and development status of a child are overlooked when examining the effects of the addictive process. For example, in my family, when my mother's addiction reached its peak, my oldest brother was at the developmental age where he was preparing to leave home. The addiction helped push him out of the house. However, I was the youngest of the family, in junior high, and couldn't leave home. Both of us are children of addiction, but the addictive process didn't affect us in the same way.

Numerous factors need to be considered when determining the effects of addiction on children. Following is a list of questions to think about when determining how any child has been affected by addiction.

# Questions to Consider When Thinking about How the Addictive Process May Affect Children

1. What was the child's development status when the addiction started to affect the functioning of the family?

2. What was the child's development status when the addiction was at its worst?

3. What is the sex of the child? The sex of the addicted parent?

4. How hard did the parents work to protect the child from the effects of the addictive process?

5. What personal resources did the child have to fight the effects of the addictive process?

6. Did anyone outside the family take on the duties of the addictive parent?

7. What resources did the family have to fight the addictive process?

8. What was the relationship between the parent and the child like before the addiction started?

9. If there are siblings, how did each deal with the addiction?

10. How was addiction viewed in the child's culture?

11. What type of personality did the addicted parent take on when high or drunk? When sober?

**Fig. 11**

## How Addiction Affects Children at Different Stages of Development

Psychologist Erik Erikson defined eight stages of psycho-social development that all human beings go through from birth to old age. Focusing on the first five stages of development, concerning children and adolescents, we'll examine how addiction may affect the children in each of these stages when the addictive process is at its worst. The following chart lists Erikson's main development stages, the psychological tasks for each stage, and their outcomes if the tasks are successfully completed.* For example, in infancy, the first age group in Erikson's outline, the main task can be described as trust versus mistrust. If the infant

| Developmental Stage | Psychological Tasks | Outcomes of Each Developmental Stage |
|---|---|---|
| *Infancy* | Trust versus mistrust | Hope |
| *Early childhood* | Autonomy versus shame and doubt | Will |
| *Play age* | Initiative versus guilt | Purpose |
| *School age* | Industry versus inferiority | Competence |
| *Adolescence* | Identity versus identity confusion | Fidelity |
| *Young adulthood* | Intimacy versus isolation | Love |
| *Maturity* | Creativity versus stagnation | Care |
| *Old age* | Integrity versus despair | Wisdom |

**Fig. 12**

---

* Erik Erikson, *The Life Cycle Completed* (New York: Norton, 1985).

successfully completes this first stage, she'll be able to feel and experience a sense of hope later in life.

### Infancy and the Addictive Process: Born with a Tarnished Spoon in Your Mouth

Infancy (zero to one year) is the time in our lives when the basic cornerstones of personality are laid. We are born into a social world where our ability to establish meaningful relationships later will be critical. In *The Life Cycle Completed*, Erik Erikson writes, "At birth, the child leaves the chemical exchange of the womb for the social exchange system of their society." * The developmental goal of infancy is to develop a belief in relationships and humanity.

Our parents are our first and primary social exchange system. We unconsciously blend who they are into our being and personality as an infant. In a sense, during infancy our parents are planted in us and take seed, whether we want this or not. Their beliefs, lifestyles, and patterns of interaction become a subtle backdrop against which we will eventually judge ourselves and others.

The main job of the parent is to love, protect, and care for the infant so that the infant comes to *feel* safe. When parents create an environment absent of fear, they instill within the infant a preverbal experience and sense of trust and safety.

Most parents willingly give of themselves to help the infant develop. The more love the parent is able to express to the child, the more trust the infant feels. A sense of connectedness develops. "Parents must not only have certain

---

* Perhaps addiction is an attempt to leave the social exchange system and reenter a womblike chemical exchange process.

ways of guiding by prohibition and permission; they must also be able to represent to the child a deep, an almost somatic conviction that there is *meaning* to what they are doing," writes Erikson.

When relationship needs of infants go unfulfilled, they may become reluctant to move out into the world when they grow older. Infants born into full-blown addictive family environments are born into families that oppose nurturing relationships. These infants develop into some of the most damaged children in our society. If a child has known nothing but the addictive way since the first day of life, how can that child possibly find hope as a teen?

When these infants cry, no one comes because the adults are passed out on the couch. If an addicted parent does answer, the infant may be yelled at or told to shut up and go back to sleep. If the parent is sober in the morning and feels shameful for neglecting the infant, he may suddenly coo the infant for hours. Such random care makes it nearly impossible for the infant to form any internal sense of order and influence. These infants are often screamed at because their basic human needs are seen as "burdens." They become adults who have trouble trusting in humanity, because for them there was no real humanity to trust.

Infants develop trust when they experience consistent and predictable interactions, not the inconsistency that accompanies the addictive process. Although the infant's needs get met, the care is given in an unpredictable fashion. Instead of being fed at appropriate and consistent times during the day, the infant is fed whenever the alcoholic or addicted parents are available and responsible.

Infants continually absorb the tonal quality of their environment. Although they are unable to understand their surroundings, they take it all in: the sounds, the looks, the positive or negative energy, the intensity of voices, smiles or frowns, the brightness or darkness of the world. The abnormally drastic and intense mood shifts addicts experience are hard for most adults to understand. Can you imagine an infant trying to do so? Betty was born into an addicted family:

> For me, from day one, the world has been an unsafe place. I trust no one and expect no one to trust me. The first thing I do whenever I enter into any situation is feel it out. I'm great at this. I can tell who or what I'm to become, and then I become it. I needed to do this in my family to survive. The better I do this, the safer I feel. People are selfish and only care about themselves. If you know this and accept this, you can use it to your advantage.

Again, children who grow up in addictive homes become mistrustful and lacking in faith as a result of the chaotic and random administration of their needs, as well as the negative climate and tone of the addictive process.

It's vitally important that infants learn the natural and *consistent* rhythms of give-and-take that occur in loving relationships. This allows infants to develop trust in their families as well as humanity. In *The Life Cycle Completed*, Erikson states that when infants are exposed to such behaviors at this stage, they become adults with a good sense of "faith and realism."

### Early Childhood and the Addictive Process:
### The Creation of a Shame-Based Personality

In early childhood (one to two years) children strive to exert some self-control while developing a sense of themselves as separate from others. As the child's self develops, his personality emerges. In early childhood, children become increasingly aware of their personality and how it fits and clashes with the world around them. When children shout the word *no* at this age, they are demonstrating their ongoing awareness of their individuality. They're starting the work of finding and making a place for themselves in their families and world. Ideally, children exit this period with a sense of pride and self-esteem.

Early childhood is the season when we begin learning how to care for and discipline ourselves. Caring for oneself involves gaining control over one's impulses. During this time, we enter into a struggle to gain control over our muscle system. We must learn many physical tasks and skills: walking, running, carrying heavy objects, pouring milk, eating with utensils, and so on. As we accomplish these tasks, we gain a sense of self-control that contains the seeds of our self-esteem and self-confidence. As we become more skilled and confident, our world broadens. Our successes bring with them new struggles.

Struggles around priorities emerge; even as small children we have to make choices. We have to decide what we want to eat, what game we want to play, which parent we want to talk to. In this way, we sort out impulses from our desires and needs. We face the human dilemma of endless vision with limited choices.

Children at this age begin to experience the drives for pleasure, power, and meaning inside them. They know what piece of candy they want for pleasure; how effective temper tantrums can be to gain power; and that some of the things Mom and Dad share with them are important. Children start learning, with the help of their parents, how to prioritize their drives. Children must learn how to live with all three drives. How parents deal with their child's emerging drives is critical. Do the parents view the child as an animal whose spirit must be broken, often through physical force, or do they view the child as a potential Abraham Lincoln or Martin Luther King Jr., whose spirit must be respected and guided with love and care?

### Ethical Parenting

In early childhood, the social relationship between parents and children comes into full bloom. How the parent provides for the child's physical needs is critical. The child is like a sponge ready to soak up knowledge and values. The more ethical and loving the parenting, the more the child comes to embrace and enjoy the tasks of learning and acquiring skills, which will help her learn more.

Ethical parenting combines meaning, thought, and disciplined action; it is based on principles, not power or pleasure. This kind of parenting is informed and directed by a purpose: to encourage children to grow and develop to the best of their abilities. It involves as much change and sacrifice for the parent, maybe more, as it does for the child.

Ethical parenting is scary and challenging, but also comforting to children. Children see their parents struggling with the same issues that they face, only on a more developed level. Watching their parents work to control their own impulses and connect to spiritual principles, the children feel the stability of their parents' values. Children are more willing to follow a parent who is led by principles than one who is led by impulses.

In my work, I've had the privilege of sitting in on many conversations between children and parents. One I particularly remember was between my client and his father, whom my client greatly respected. Knowing that his grandfather had been a violent alcoholic, my client wanted to know how his father had become such a competent, good parent. The father said:

> I learned early, before you were born, that most anyone could father a child. This my father did. But it takes work—laborious work—to be a parent. This my father couldn't do. To be a parent is an honor that must be earned. When your mother placed you in my hands that first time, I knew I wanted that honor more than anything. Nothing was going to stop me from being your parent, not even myself.

## Holding On, Letting Go

In life, we're constantly learning new ideas and acquiring and letting go of people and objects. We choose this, let go of that. One of the most important skills we'll ever develop concerns what to hold on to and what to let go of. Life is an endless refining of this skill.

Letting go involves surrender. As small children, we learn to surrender our impulses to the guidance of parents. At this phase of our development, we don't possess enough knowledge and power to resist even if we wanted to. Thus, our parents will teach us by their example. What our parents have surrendered their lives to is vastly important; in turn many children will follow suit.

Watching how our parents live their lives and following their lead is how we develop our own belief systems and how we learn to rank and prioritize pleasure, power, and meaning. And this is how the addictive process is transferred and embedded into children whose parents are afflicted with this illness. If parents structure their lives around pleasure and power, their children most often assign the same importance to these two drives. However, if parents structure their lives around meaning, then their children will learn to center their lives on principles and truth. Children learn to recognize what is truth and what is false. As we mature, we start to see the principles behind our parents' actions, and we learn that actions should indeed be led by principles.

If we're taught to hold on to that which weakens and deadens our spirits and to let go of that which nourishes our spirits, we're set up for a life of misery and shame. Children of addicts continually watch their parents make this basic mistake. Addiction is an illness of wrong choices. It's a lifestyle of denying that one has made a wrong choice. Of course, when a child's role model—the parent—makes the wrong choices again and again, it's extremely difficult for the child to make the right choices.

If a child has lived a "normal" life up to this point and then is exposed to the addictive process, the hope that they developed during the infancy stage is jeopardized. Children may then instinctively build defenses to protect themselves and their hope against the addictive process; this protects them from their parents. In early childhood, children living in addictive homes are attracted to and repulsed by their parents. Shame often resolves this conundrum. On an emotional leave, they become what they perceive is wrong. They come to *feel* wrong.

### Mutual Regulation

During early childhood, both parent and child need to be involved in what Erikson calls *mutual regulation*. This means a mutual give-and-take in the parent-child relationship. If both the parent and the child regulate themselves and develop a rhythm between each other, an internal sense of order unfolds. A sense of comfort with order and restraining one's impulses develops internally. Discipline and suppression of impulses start to feel right and make sense. Sometimes you control yourself because it's what you need, and sometimes you do it for those you love because it's what they need. Sometimes you're quiet because you want to be; sometimes you're quiet because Mom has a headache and she wants you to be. Sometimes a parent reads a book to the child because the parent likes the book; sometimes the parent reads a book to the child for the *hundredth* time because the child likes it. In all these examples, the relationship is reciprocal and interactive, not controlled by one person.

If both child and parents are involved in this process of mutual regulation, mutual vulnerability develops. The parent and child share their successes, mistakes, and failures with each other. One parent described mutuality like this: "I know my son will be changed and influenced by me; I hope he knows someday how much he has changed and influenced me."

Mutual vulnerability is a fundamental building block of intimacy. It involves making room for *all* parts of each other's humanity. In a mutually vulnerable relationship, I allow myself to be changed by you, and you allow yourself to be changed by me. Without mutual vulnerability, intimacy cannot grow and thrive.

In addictive families, mutual vulnerability rarely occurs. Addiction, like other major illnesses, follows its own course and will not be diverted. The addicted person cannot share openly with other family members, as this would endanger the addict's continued drug use. As children of addiction grow out of early childhood, they feel as if they have no influence or importance in the family and no need to regulate themselves. Jill talks about this in relation to her mother's drinking:

> Some of my earliest thoughts seem to be about my mother and her drinking. I remember or feel as if I remember thinking, "Why does she act this way? I've asked her to stop and she won't. Am I wrong?" I would ask Mom to stop drinking, and she would yell at me and have another drink. After a while I felt as if what I said didn't matter. I shut up and gave up. If she didn't have to control herself, then I didn't have to either. If being right didn't matter, then why bother? I gave up. It wasn't until I was forty-one that I stopped giving up and shutting up. I was right then, and I'm still right today.

Addiction disrupts any sense of order in the family. Randomness and chaos are the norm. Consequently, children feel or sense that they have little influence. This causes or deepens the shame a child may be feeling. Then, one's insides feel like sand, always shifting and being blown around as the winds of addiction change.

### Play Age and the Addictive Process:
### Playing with One's Sense of Purpose

According to Erikson, the goal of this stage (two to five years) is for the child to "emerge with a sense of unbroken initiative." This means that the child is able to stay focused on a task until it is completed and to experience pride in achieving the goal. If the child attains his goal at this stage, the resulting sense of unbroken initiative is later transformed into healthy ambition and independence. The child will feel guided by a sense of purpose.

Under normal conditions, by this stage a child will clearly see herself as separate from others. Play age is also the time when children begin to experience themselves as part of a group, such as the family, day care, preschool, or "club." If children develop properly during this stage, they will later see themselves as part of larger groups in their community and the world. They'll feel a greater sense of belonging to humanity.

A common desire for children in the play age is to be adultlike, to be "big" and more in control. At this time, children learn about the basics of power. When they dress up in Mom's high-heeled shoes or Dad's tie and sport coat, they are exploring the idea of power. For children, power means safety. When they slay dragons, they are slaying their own fears. In a safe home and environment, children can run to the protective comfort of their parents when the dragons get too big.

Children in addictive families also desire power—to be big enough—but not to fight dragons. They want to fight and defeat the demon of addiction in their families. Of course, the child must fail. When confronted by the power of the addictive process, children of addicts often feel ashamed, angry, and guilty about their smallness or lack of power. Since they don't yet have the capacity to reason that they're not responsible, they feel inadequate. According to Erikson, the child whose development needs don't get met during this time may end up feeling guilty.

It's natural for children at this age to feel that their parents are scary. Parents are so much larger and more powerful than they are. In healthy homes, children usually take comfort in their parents' power. They have it to fall back on when they reach their own limitations. They can ask Mom or Dad to open a jar or to reach up to the top shelf. These children are rarely made to feel ashamed or burdened by their size. Their families exert ethical power that's controlled and directed. Children of addicted parents, on the other hand, can feel haunted by their parents' power. Jason talks about how he experienced power as a child in a family of addicts:

> I often dreamed of being able to become as big as I wanted, anytime I wanted. It was my favorite dream. The dream was always the same. Someone in my family would be chasing me. I would turn to face them and start to grow. I grew twice their size; then I grew bigger than the houses in our neighborhood. I would look down on them and laugh. Now they were scared and were running away from me. I would just stand there laughing at them. In my waking life, I was always scared, but not in my dreams.

Children in addictive families rarely experience the use of power as ethical or just. What's "right" is often determined not by values but by the parent's moods or level of intoxication. These children quickly learn that "might makes right."

In this stage of child development, children enter the verbal world; they begin to understand things without having to see them. Ideas and concepts are becoming embedded into their beings. Although they can't understand abstract concepts as well as children in the next stage, their conscience develops during this stage through dependence on a parent or an adult figure. "Only as a dependent does man develop conscience and it is only through conscience that man can come to depend on himself," writes Erikson in *The Life Cycle Completed.*

Imagine being forced to depend on someone you find disgusting and repulsive. Who wants to be dependent on a practicing addict? No one. Not even a small child who must. This child, then, develops a conscience by being dependent on himself and what other adults—teacher, day care provider, and so on—tell him. This child may even adopt the value system of the culture at large. Television can become the parent and teacher for children of addicts. It teaches them how to act and solve problems—which on television often means violence. Television may only reinforce what they are learning at home.

If a child doesn't develop a conscience based on meaning and principles, she may develop a more primitive, cruel, burdened, and uncompromising conscience rooted in raw power. As this child grows up, she develops a conscience based on a self-righteous attitude instead of morality. Self-righteousness is about power; it views all ethical issues as being either right or wrong.

This child will develop a sense of who is right and who is wrong or who should be blamed. Such a sense is critical to survival in an addictive family, where being "right" gives you more power and authority to blame others.

I once had a client, a woman in her forties, who came in after she had been involved in a very self-righteous group for many years. It was only after the leader of this group disappeared and left the country with the group's funds that she questioned her dependence. She realized that, as a result of growing up with severely alcoholic parents, she never developed a mature conscience and was prey to authoritarian, self-righteous people. "I wanted to be so much better than my parents," she said. "I guess I wanted to make up for them, but I was terribly resentful. I eventually became so judgmental that I couldn't see straight. I couldn't see that I had hooked up with someone who was as amoral as my parents were."

Many children of addicts overcompensate for their parents, trying to make up for their parents or prove that they never cared or needed them, which of course isn't true. If the child overcompensates by seeking power instead of meaning, he will create a lifestyle of holding on to the wrong things and letting go of the right things.

When children of addicts leave the play stage with no sense of purpose, they compensate by developing an exaggerated sense of self-importance. Teens who have an exaggerated sense of self and who lack a genuine conscience based on values and principles often act out by having sex at a premature age, because they want to feel "big" like an adult. They don't see how they're still children themselves. They may join a gang to feel grown-up, pretending it won't damage—or end their future.

### School Age and the Addictive Process: Being One Down

During these years (five to twelve years) children naturally become more independent from their families in some very important ways. Some children of addicts, however, may hesitate to step out on their own because they believe they need to stay home and watch over their addicted parents. Mary Ann remembers how she dreaded going to school and leaving her mother unattended at home:

> As I look back at my school-age years, I missed a lot of school. Not really because I was sick but because my mom was sick. Some days I just couldn't leave her home alone. So I pretended I was sick. I know in the state she was in, she could have passed out with a cigarette in her hand and burnt the house and herself up. The days I did go to school I felt terror every time I heard fire sirens. Often I'd call home during lunch just to hear Mom answer the phone.

Other children of addictive families may feel extraordinary relief to live apart, if only for a school day, from their families. Anne remembers how excited she felt about going to school:

> I couldn't wait to get to school. I was always the first one at the bus stop. I signed up for after-school activities as soon as I could. School was wonderful. It saved my life. Some days, on my way home, I might cry. I knew what awaited me: anger, fights, poverty, and my dad's cocaine.

During school-age years, children feel proud and gain self-esteem from accomplishing certain tasks. For some children of addicts, as Bob explains, school becomes all-consuming, the only way to feel competent in anything:

> I loved school. I would get assignments, do them, and feel good. "Extra Credit" became my nick-name. As I got older, I would research and write papers on things that interested me. At home, Dad drank, and he and Mom would argue endlessly about money, kids, and his drinking. By studying and working at school, I could numb out the rage and pain bottled up inside of me. Looking back, it is no surprise that I went into a deep depression when I was laid up in the hospital for three months. As I lay there in a body cast, thoughts and feelings about my growing up that I had drowned out came rushing up. I itched terribly!

Children at this age are also learning how to be social and participate in their peer groups. Children of addicts feel inferior to others and isolated and join whatever group will have them. Sometimes they become the leaders of their groups to compensate for their powerlessness and low self-esteem. It lets them feel good and in control. The groups that many of these children join are made up of other lost children. The leader then becomes a "pretend parent," who can tell them how to act and live. As long as they are part of the group, life seems meaningful. They get another chance, though a distorted one, at achieving a sense of family.

It is critical that school-age children of addicts explore new avenues where they might create meaningful lives for themselves. Many children of addicts learn to detach from their families in helpful ways during these years. This may continue and increase in the adolescent years.

### Resilient Children

Some children of addictive families may develop into what Emmy Werner calls *resilient children*. In a thirty-year study, Werner found that nearly one-third of the children of alcoholics and addicts grew up to have normal, productive lives. In her book *Vulnerable but Invincible*, she talked of how resilient children found support outside of their families. "Resilient children . . . tended to be well liked by their classmates and had at least one close friend and usually several. They relied on an informal network of neighbors, peers, and elders for counsel and support. They seem to make school a home away from home, a refuge from a disordered household. For others, emotional support came from a church group, a youth leader in YMCA or YWCA or a favorite minister." Resilient children possess the ability to see what is happening, distance themselves from the worst of the craziness—at least emotionally—and self-repair the damage inflicted on them. Resilient children are able to stay connected to principles of betterment and find ways to keep their humanity alive. Why one child can do this and another can't isn't clear.

It is clear, however, that resilient children sometimes pay an emotional price for finding this humanity outside the family. They often feel that they've betrayed their families. In fact, they have—and must. In order to survive, they've separated from the addictive process and the deterioration at home. Linda recalls the guilt she felt about liking school and her teachers more than anyone in her immediate family:

> I found a wonderful new home in school. My friends became my siblings and my teachers became my parents. My mother would say, "You love that place more than you love us." Inside, I felt terrible. She was right. I did. When I felt guilty, I'd try to spend more time at home, but I'd soon go back and spend most of my spare time at school.

### The Ways of the World

Between the ages of five and twelve, children are stepping out and learning the ways of the world, which are different from the ways of intimacy. Home life ideally offers a counterbalance to worldly ways. Home is where our spirits should be cared for and nurtured. The home should be organized around meaning, since the outside world is mainly organized around power. If their home life doesn't provide meaning and support, children will naturally feel a greater pull out into the world.

Stepping out into the world at this age includes dealing with group politics. Granted, politics for children this young take place in a very small world, but it is nevertheless a world in which they must begin to negotiate their needs. Their social interactions are often based more on pleasure and power than on meaning. Popularity doesn't always come from how well you live your life, but from things you have, your appearance, your clothing, and how much money you or your parents have.

In the social world, people develop methods and tactics to get what they want. There is intrigue and maneuvering within and among groups. For children of addicts, this can be either comfortable or uncomfortable. A sense of discomfort may come from feeling inferior and one down, mainly from the shame they carry around. Or it may feel comfortable being in a power-based system where everyone is your size.

If children of addicts find comfort in the social politics of school and its subgroups, they have an area where they can excel. Often, because they are coming from a system organized around addiction, they may handle the social politics much better than the other children. They may become quite popular with other kids because of the comfort they can demonstrate around power. Rachel recalls just such a time:

> When I started school, life got easy. Most of the kids were scared and nervous, but I moved in with great ease. I was always the leader of any social group. I knew how to get what I wanted or what my friends wanted, because I had watched my father manipulate and intimidate our family for years. I now had a place to compete where I could win. I loved it and I blossomed, but I was also as mean as my father if I didn't get what I wanted. When it came time for me to separate from the group and be alone, I felt small, alone, and afraid. My friends became my family. It is still that way today; I feel comfortable when I'm out with friends, but stepping

into my home, where I should be comfortable, scares me. I use my home just to sleep at, not as a place to brings friends to.

### Adolescence and the Addictive Process: A Ship without a Rudder

The goal of adolescence (twelve to nineteen years) is consolidation. In this stage, adolescents begin to form their own model of life from what they've experienced or learned. This model will direct and guide them out of adolescence. Adolescence is also a time of enormous changes for one's body and mind as well as one's belief and value system.

Normally, one enters adolescence as a child and leaves as a young adult. Children of addicts, however, may start adolescence as adults—at the age of twelve.

In most cases adolescents crave *and* fear the new world that awaits them. They must solve the paradox they have become—a child adult. They feel they deserve all the rights and privileges that come with being an adult, yet often behave in childlike ways. For example, my friend had an argument with her fourteen-year-old daughter who wanted to stay overnight at her friend's house without any parental supervision. In the middle of the argument, this woman's daughter asked her to please wash her stuffed bear so she could take it with her overnight. The bear got cleaned, but the slumber party ended up at my friend's house, much to the regret of her daughter who wanted the privileges of an adult *and* her teddy bear.

Although adolescents need parenting, *they* struggle against it. They naturally reject their parents, yet can't wait to be around them. They crave familiarity and routines while rebelling against anything that smacks of familiarity.

They need and want help, yet act as if they don't. During this time, teens are asking important questions, such as "Who am I?" and "Who will I be?" Parents can be a hard reminder to teens that they haven't matured and are still dependent, like a child, on their families.

Parents are critically important in helping adolescents answer identity questions and become more grounded in who they are. They can encourage teens to take more risks and become more independent. Adolescents watch how their parents follow their values and principles during stormy times. Teens see parents as the ship of values being tested in storms, before the teens themselves go out on their own long voyage. They need to test parents and then see how they resolve the test. Adolescents are determining whether their parents' values and principles are just nice phrases or something durable that provides true guidance during tough times. Children of drug addicts or alcoholics likely witness their parents abandoning their principles of betterment.

All teens need routine and predictability at home, yet teens in addictive family systems will only find chaos. They hope their parents will help them solve problems, but see them using crisis as an excuse to get drunk. The adolescents' natural instability is the most stable thing surrounding them. Instead of forming an identity, they are most often reacting and negatively adjusting to an unnatural situation. They are ships without a rudder. They end up in ports into which the winds of family addiction have blown them. Not surprising, they connect with other rudderless ships that have been blown into the same harbor.

This is the heart of the problem for adolescents in addictive families. The parents they need to fall back on for guidance and values are not solid—and they may not even be there, physically or psychologically. Many of these adolescents are raising themselves.

What happens when adolescents in need of adult guidance find their addictive parents more childlike than they are? What happens when adolescents seeking meaningful discussion return to a home of denial? Who and what are they to believe in? It's no surprise that many of these adolescents seek comfort and guidance from their peer group, gangs, other children from addictive families, and the pop culture, which includes commercials, movies, actors, and rock stars. Although some of this is natural for all adolescents, it is absolutely necessary for those in addictive families.

It's important to feel at ease about one's own understanding of self, since this understanding will evolve as one ages. Adolescents, then, need to develop a solid sense of identity *and* the ability to question themselves and add new aspects to their identity. This skill, which we need throughout life, allows us to grow and change without losing a core of principles and values.

Adolescence can be a wonderful time for transformation. Although we have experienced great transformations since birth, as we will throughout life, adolescence is the first period where choices can influence the transformation. It is the first period of growth where we are generally aware of our transformation. We feel our egos, sense our spirits, and try to integrate the ways of the world into both of them. We must begin to stand for and with something.

Meaning is what holds relationships together and brings joy to our lives. By the end of adolescence, ideally, we see this and have moved toward a life based on meaning and the principles of betterment. Children of addicts, unfortunately, have been taught that power and pleasure bring true satisfaction in life. They often leave adolescence and embark on a life path that leads to broken dreams, broken marriages, and broken lives.

## Conclusion

In this chapter, we've looked at how addiction may interfere with the developmental tasks of children, from birth to young adulthood. The illness of addiction can handicap children by making them feel inadequate. For them, intimacy is a burden, not a blessing. These children have been taught by the example of their addicted parents that power and pleasure are more important than meaning, which is a terribly false and destructive illusion. Instead of learning the skills to change formless love into created love, they are learning negative skills and attitudes of mistrust and suspicion, and how to seek comfort from all the wrong sources.

Next we'll discuss how families can and do recover. Here's a preview of what's to come: The way for the addictive family to accomplish a radical change based on meaning rather than on power or pleasure is to temporarily borrow a new support and value system until they can reclaim their own. The family's recovery depends on setting up a new system of interaction.

# PART 4

# RECOVERY

# Introduction to Part 4

### Scene 4

Maggie Jensen had cut herself deeper than ever before when she fell in the kitchen. The doctor smelled alcohol on her breath, checked her chart, and saw that she had a history of similar injuries. He contacted a social worker to interview her husband, Ted, and son, David. After reviewing information and Maggie's elevated blood alcohol level, everyone agreed chemical dependency treatment was needed. Maggie offered much less resistance than Ted had imagined she would.

Much has changed in the fourteen short days since Ted and David took Maggie to the emergency room. Now they sit in a circle with other families. David tries to figure out which people in the group are addicts and which are family members like him. He imagines the addicts are the ones who hang their heads low or hold them a bit too high, as if to challenge everyone in the room.

David can't decide whether he likes this place or not. The people seem nice, the counselors both gentle and tough, but having to sit in front of his mother and tell her how her drinking has hurt him seems ridiculous and impossible. Yet the counselors have insisted he do this during family week.

Ted notices that at times he has felt a strange peace and yet whenever they mention the word alcoholic, he

grows uneasy. He likes and dislikes hearing other families talk. He imagines his own family, David and Maggie, and wavers between believing they are all lost and believing they may recover a semblance of strength and hope. Ted is scared.

Maggie feels intensely bitter and angry toward Ted and David. What they said to the social worker resulted in her being labeled "alcoholic." She clearly and frequently lets Ted know she is not happy. Yet she occasionally finds herself listening carefully to the lectures and looking forward to hearing certain others in her treatment group, especially one woman about her age who's been in treatment for three-and-a-half weeks now. Maggie finds herself strangely attracted to her and her story. The woman has a son about the same age as David, and she seems to have a peace around her that Maggie hasn't known for years. How could she have gone through what Maggie is going through and still have peace? How strange this new world is, Maggie thinks.

## The Family as It Enters Recovery

So what does a family entering recovery look like? Think of addiction as a hurricane bearing down on the coasts of Florida, Georgia, and the Carolinas. Addictive families might be cities and towns along the coast battered by the storm as it passes. Some families take a direct hit by the illness. Some couples divorce. Maybe an older child or children leave home, never to return, and write their families off as an unpleasant memory. Most families experience intense psychological and emotional damage from the storm and will need to start an extensive rebuilding process. The good news is that when families work conscientiously in a program, many recover, rebuild, and regain the trust, fun, intimacy, and love that was lost or damaged by the fury of addiction.

Unlike a hurricane, the effects of addiction are prolonged, insidious, and difficult to pinpoint. Some family members may have escaped the full impact of the storm, left home before the worst of it hit, joined the service, found jobs or schools in distant cities, or even married. Others may have found adequate psychological shelter at church, school, or the neighbors down the street.

Many families believe that everything will be fine now that the addicted person has stopping using drugs or alcohol: "We will talk easily again; we won't be afraid of each other anymore; the tension will go away," they think. For years, a family might have pleaded, "Just stop drinking. That's all I ask!" Now that the drinking has stopped, however, they find that the resentments are still there, along with the mistrust, distance, and loneliness. Now that they don't have to constantly worry about the addict getting drunk or high, family members have a chance to experience the depth of the damage caused by the illness. It's out there for everyone to see. In the book *Alcoholics Anonymous* we read: "We feel the elimination of our drinking is but a beginning." The reality is that most often recovery is long, hard, and wonderful.

The addict may get upset that the family does not instantly accept and trust him. But how many times has the addict promised to stop before? It's normal for family members to wonder, "How long will it last?" The family is scared: "Will he be able to stay sober? How can I open my heart to someone who has hurt me so much? He may get drunk again. How can I become vulnerable, speak openly, when the last time I did that I was yelled at?" Families cannot and should not immediately take down their defense mechanisms. They need to see that sobriety is holding.

What can families reasonably expect when their loved ones enter treatment or pursue recovery in a Twelve Step program? In this section, we will discuss the phases of recovery and what a family can expect in these phases. Here are some of the general characteristics of the addictive family as it enters treatment:

- a genuine desire and hope that all will be fine now, tempered by distrust
- a collective loneliness
- hopefulness and cynicism
- hurt, anger, and fear
- high levels of mistrust of even positive changes
- use of a defense system created to survive addiction
- skepticism about the future
- focus on short-term needs and issues
- reliance on drive for power instead of drive for meaning

- major issues with trust
- role confusion

## Restoring Love

We have followed Maggie, Ted, and David through the stages of addiction, and now they sit on the edge of a new world. We have also seen the destructive power of addiction. The love that the Jensens once experienced appears to be lost. As we have seen, addiction is an illness that causes individuals to betray the spiritual principles that create love. With continual betrayal of the principles of betterment, love can only decay. The family members that once loved spending Sundays together now plan separate activities. The family that used to laugh and joke at the dinner table now eats in silence. The couple can no longer plan a future. It is terrifying to see love dissolve. How will it end?

Hollywood tells us love can fix all things. Human love, however, does have limits. Love alone can't heal cancer, heart disease, diabetes, or addiction. Recovery and healing from addiction takes a community of professionals, therapists, friends, those in recovery circles, and the entire family. On a personal level, recovery is about reclaiming our lives from the addictive process. It is about getting back and restoring the love that was lost to addiction.

## The Recovery Bind

Families entering recovery are in a bind: that which helped the family survive—an overdeveloped defense system—works against the recovery process. In the past, members of an addictive family learned to be independent, reduce their needs, disconnect from their emotions, and deny and live with high levels of pain, abuse, and neglect. These defenses helped them survive as a family. They relied heavily on these defense mechanisms to get through any given day and to survive the insanity of addiction. Now, in recovery, these behaviors only increase their problems. The family's survival depends on members learning new communication skills.

In addiction and early recovery, the family's survival depended on defending themselves, not examining themselves. For example, blaming others is a very good survival tool during addiction. Blaming someone else, like the addict, effectively diverts some of your own painful feelings and keeps your power base intact. If you are the addict coming home drunk and your wife is waiting up, you might yell, "Don't you dare blame me. If you show me half the care my friends at the bar show me, I'd never drink again." Of course, your wife, though angry, half believes you because she knows how little she cares. So she walks away feeling horrible, wondering if she indeed is to blame.

Blaming allows the addict to escape responsibility. It may even ease some of his guilt, intolerable shame, and self-loathing. This in turn may allow him to survive in the addictive family, to keep him at least coming home at night. Once an addict is clean and sober, however, blaming only keeps him and other family members from true recovery.

## The Challenges of Recovery

Recovery challenges individuals and families to shift from being reactive to being responsible. It challenges them to set aside egos and risk honest involvement with others. All family members will be challenged to put aside their

# The Pleasure, Power, Connection, and Meaning Framework

### DRIVE FOR MEANING
(Domain of TRANSFORMATION)

*WITHIN THIS REALM WE FIND:*

our humanity

a desire to live as part and member of a community

the ability to create relationships centered around principles of betterment

continued connection to principles of betterment increases self-esteem, self-love

### DRIVE FOR POWER
(Domain of CONTROL)

*WITHIN THIS REALM WE FIND:*

a desire to be and become powerful

a desire to have the power to overcome that which would destroy us

a desire to be in control and to lead

self-confidence

a predator mentality

### DRIVE FOR PLEASURE
(Domain of AVOIDANCE)

*WITHIN THIS REALM WE FIND:*

a desire and ability to feel pleasure

a desire to please and bring pleasure to others

an attraction to live in a trancelike state

an attraction to concept of transformation

ability to feel limitless at times

## Drive Development of Person in a Twelve Step Recovery Program

**A.**

When a person enters recovery, the drives for power and pleasure are in a leadership role. Over time, by the use of surrender and discipline, the person's drive for meaning is reestablished into a leadership role.

**B.**

In early recovery, the personal support system in combination with spiritual principles creates a balance of the addicted person's drives.

**C.**

Growth through recovery means a reintegration of spiritual principles into the person's life and lifestyle. Spiritual principles are regularly used to solve the issues and problems of life.

**Fig. 13:** The recovery process begins with the establishing, or reestablishing, of spiritual principles into the person's life: honesty, acceptance, surrender, and so on. As this happens, a rebalancing of the drives occurs and growth is achieved. The person's drive for power and drive for pleasure again become subordinate to spiritual principles and the needs of intimate relationships. The drive for meaning now leads while working in concert with the drives for power and pleasure.

anger and explore new communication methods. No more yelling or pointing fingers. Recovery asks everyone again to believe and rely on spiritual principles (see figure 13). It may start with the principle of honesty: "Yes, I don't trust you, and I don't know if I can."

Recovery challenges co-addicts and addicts alike to live a life not organized around addiction but health. New questions arise: "How do I go to the family picnic and respectfully say no to Uncle Frank when he offers me a beer? How do I act? What do I say when I see Dad looking as if he wants to go drink again? How do I trust my daughter after she has acted so irresponsibly?" Recovery will provide answers to these types of questions and more.

Self-regulation is another major challenge in recovery. Family members must now learn to contain those impulses they used to act out and instead redirect their energy. Before, when your son came home late, you may have yelled, "Where have you been?" In recovery, you're challenged to contain your impulse to yell and lecture, and think of "better" ways to handle a situation that will preserve your dignity. Support groups can help. You'll need to be willing to analyze and control your behavior and be willing to forgive others. The family must establish a system of communication based on dialogue instead of raging and belittling monologues.

The recovering family will be challenged to pick up, use, and become skillful with many new tools. Some of these tools require continuous sobriety, regular attendance in support groups, personal reflection, self-accountability, prayer, sponsorship, and service.

## Responsibility

Responsibility and blame are major issues in early recovery. Although many people believe the disease concept of addiction lets addicts escape responsibility for the harm they've caused, this is not true. (When attorneys use the disease concept to get a client off a charge related to alcohol or other drugs, they're distorting the concept.) Recovery is about the addict and her family taking responsibility.

Responsibility pushes the person into ownership, into guilt instead of shame. A responsible addict in recovery might say, "Yes, I am guilty of having an illness that has brought you great pain." A responsible family member might say, "Yes, I'm guilty of hating you because you have an illness." They both might say, "We must work to restore our family."

Responsibility is one of the first issues that family members encounter in recovery. Each person will be asked to take responsibility for how he or she has dealt with the addiction in the past. Parents may need to take responsibility for yelling and screaming at their addicted daughter. The wife may need to take responsibility for the affair she had just to get even with her drunken husband. In order for the family to recover, members must become honest and accountable for their behavior. When counselors or sponsors say, "Stop blaming yourself and get over it," they're pushing the person past the blame and into responsibility. Instead of blaming ourselves and others, we are asked to be kinder to our families. Instead of feeling sorry for ourselves, we are encouraged to put aside our self-pity and ask how our family members are doing. Instead of blaming ourselves, it might be better just to go load the dishwasher or take a long enjoyable walk.

Family members must take responsibility for their actions and then do what is needed to correct the situation, unlike Brian, who accepted blame for all the misery within his family:

> I was so shameful and apologetic when I got to treatment. I'd sit with my family and just say, "I'm sorry, I'm sorry. Please, please forgive me." This counselor told me to get down off my cross and use the wood to build a boat to get my family and myself out of the swamp we were in. I was shocked that he could be so unsympathetic. He told me to stop indulging in my own pain and start working for the courage to hear the pain of my family. I told him I knew how badly I had hurt my family. He said maybe I did, but would I be willing to stop my whining and make room for them to talk about it? That put smiles on my family members' faces. He was right. It took me time. I didn't know how much pain they had felt.

Fighting over who is to blame will not further the family's recovery. Blaming blocks us from owning our behavior and attitudes and realizing that addiction is an illness and not anything one chooses. Families dealing with cancer don't sit around trying to figure out who is to blame. But with addiction they do. Sandy and her family had at least one thing in common going into treatment—everyone thought they were at fault:

> I remember that first week of treatment and my fear that it would be established that all the problems in the family were my fault. I was waiting for the group to say, "Sandy, as the addict, you need to see that you are the cause of all the pain in your

family." Years later I found out that everyone else in the family had that same fear. Mom told me she was waiting to hear, "Gladys, if you had been a better mom and watched over her better, Sandy would never have gotten into drugs." Dad was waiting to hear, "Glenn, if you had just spent more time with your daughter instead of so much time with your career, she would never have used drugs." My younger brother was sure that it was his fault because he teased me. We all laughed and joked that probably Sam, our mutt dog, was saying to himself, "If only I hadn't barked so much, this wouldn't have happened." We are all so glad to be away from the blaming that became a way of life.

## Stages of Recovery

The family recovery process can be divided into three stages. Though there are no clear beginnings and endings to these stages and they may overlap, families will deal with different tasks and issues depending on where they are in the recovery process. In early recovery, a family will require more honesty and tolerance; in middle recovery, understanding and acceptance; and finally in late recovery, love.

# CHAPTER 8

# EARLY RECOVERY:
# HONESTY
# AND TOLERANCE

The first task of recovery for families is to admit they are powerless over the illness of addiction—to admit they are no more able to control addiction and its consequences with willpower and determination than they are any other illness. Admitting powerlessness will mean different things for different family members.

For addicts, becoming honest means taking responsibility and admitting they have an illness. They must also accept that they can't use chemicals, including alcohol, or they can't act out (if they're addicted to something other than chemicals) without severe consequences. Addicts must admit that they need to stop using or acting out in order to arrest their illness and regain control over their lives. They must take responsibility for their illness and realize that any chance they have of regaining healthy relationships with their family members depends on their abstinence and recovery. This is the reality of the illness of addiction. Addicts will need to admit that their use of alcohol or other drugs makes them unsafe to themselves, their families, friends, and others.

Co-addicts need to see and accept that they can't control the course or consequences of the illness. Staying up until three in the morning just to watch your spouse stagger in doesn't help. Yelling and demanding that the addict change has no more effect on curing addiction than screaming at a malignant tumor to stop growing. Worry and love can't cure addiction any more than they can cure heart disease. It isn't the co-addict's fault that he couldn't stop his child's addiction. I once counseled a mother who tried to convince me that her son's alcoholism was her fault because she wasn't able to breast-feed him as an infant. Every family member needs to realize that each of them is powerless over the illness of addiction.

When this happens, family members may also see that their family interactions have been centered on and controlled primarily by the addictive process—instead of the principles of betterment. They must see and believe that they're dealing with an illness more powerful than themselves. If this does not happen—if members continue to believe that they can fix, control, or gather the willpower to conquer "the problem"—they will continue living in denial. Joyce and her family began to believe in life again when they started to see and act on what was destroying their family:

> We were wowed! We knew the world was falling down around us. We just didn't know why. We all had two things in common: First, we all secretly

thought we were to blame. Second, we all thought that if we tried harder, everything would be okay someday, but someday never came. We all got more depressed. We were truly surprised when we learned that Rob had an illness. To think of his drinking as an illness made sense—we all thought of him as sick and regularly told him so, in a sarcastic way. Now this counselor was saying it was due to an illness called chemical dependency. We talked for the first time in many years that night, and no one felt or was told they were to blame. We were finally given a map that made sense. Maybe, just maybe, we dared to hope again. I slept well that night, I remember. It was the first time in years I had slept that well.

Joyce is not alone in feeling relieved to find out that addiction is an illness. This is the first step in recovery. Some people resist this and instead believe that they can control their addiction. Many family members have a hard time understanding addiction as an illness. This is often due to their hurt and anger. They mistakenly assume that to admit that addiction is an illness means they must forgive behavior they find unforgivable. Joan, a nineteen-year-old daughter of an alcoholic, describes how past resentments and hurt can get in the way of understanding addiction:

Yeah, now they tell us he has an illness. What is that supposed to mean? Am I not to be mad at him for all the nights he passed out on the dining room floor? What about the time he got up during the night and urinated in the corner because he thought it was the bathroom? Now everything is to be forgiven because he has a disease? Well, I'm

sorry—it's not going to work that way for me. If
he wants me to forgive him, he's got a lot of work
to do!

Joan's reaction is more typical than Joyce's. Joan's reaction also shows the need for tolerance and patience. Family
members feel they've been beaten up and bullied for years
by the addict. Addicts are often verbally abusive, though
they also may have been physically and sexually abusive.
Family members may want "proof"—many months of sobriety, true remorse for past harms, willingness to listen, and
commitment to a recovery program—before they let their
defenses down. This is understandable. The family wants to
see the addict invested in the recovery process before it
trusts him again. At this point, the addict's family members
need to open to *others* who can help them start their *own*
recovery process. They need to understand that though
addiction is an illness, it doesn't automatically absolve anyone of past behavior. The recovering addict will have to
regain the trust and respect of his family again. This is only
right and just.

### Need for Tolerance

Tolerance measures one's capacity to recognize and
respect the opinions, practices, and behaviors of others.
Tolerance makes room. However, by the time a family
enters recovery, members are usually fed up with all the
lying, stealing, abusing, swearing, drunkenness, late-night
phone calls, jails, dope, and so on. The family in early
recovery is often in a state of intolerance. Members are
unable or unwilling to endure any more. "Enough!" they
might shout. They are "sick and tired of being sick and
tired" and want change—now! They want their family

restored to its pre-addiction state, but intellectually they know it will take time and they need to be patient. Still, their nerves are frayed from years of lies and behavior that would scare anyone. Tolerance for a family in recovery is greatly needed but hard to come by. Support groups can help families slow down with slogans like "Easy does it" or "One day at a time."

Family members need the "room" and tolerance to work their individual recovery for a time. Mom might be frustrated, ready to blow up, and need to feel free to say: "You're on your own with supper tonight. I need to go to a meeting and get myself under control. Please help me do this and not hassle me about it." Mom might leave and return later much more serene, and everyone learns the value of being helpful and tolerant. Tolerance works to remove shame and blame from the system, while still holding people accountable for their behavior. It does not excuse or justify behavior. Tolerance doesn't seek punishment, but change. Yet the family needs to realize that some changes take time. Acquiring new attitudes and behaviors won't happen overnight.

## Parallel Recovery

The early stage of recovery is characterized by *parallel recovery*. Parallel recovery refers to each family member working separately on a personal recovery program. Parallel recovery is similar to two children sitting and playing in the same sandbox, building the same type of sandcastle, aware of the other but having little interaction except to ask for the bucket or fight over a shovel. In parallel recovery, the family members are building separate sandcastles—transforming their own lives—but not far away is the entire family.

Parallel recovery illustrates that the connections between family members are damaged and disrupted and each person needs to focus on a program of personal recovery for a period. Each family member needs to focus on developing a healthy self, so attention later can be turned to rebuilding the family. In early recovery, individuals need to accept that they have been too battered to immediately resume close, intimate relationships. Besides tolerance, time and healing are needed. Parents will need time to learn how to be parents again. Maybe a lesson as simple as spending time with the children again or as complex as guiding adolescents through dating will have to be relearned. Couples need to learn how to be together again, to discuss issues around money, and to express gratitude. Kids may need to learn to be kids again; to listen to teachers, to play with other classmates and friends, and to have sleepovers. All will have to learn how to trust again.

The task of rebuilding and healing is slow and involves many personal changes. This recovery period may last months or years, depending on everyone's involvement. A clear danger for the family in early recovery is to push too quickly for closeness and normalcy. I remember a spouse coming in angry that her husband was going to meetings three nights a week when six months ago she was praying that he would get sober. "I thought I would get him back," she said. "Well, I don't have him back. *They* have him now." She was referring to Alcoholics Anonymous as "they." She was tired of addiction and an absent husband. Though the addiction had been arrested, her husband was still absent, only now he was sitting at AA meetings instead of a bar. This woman, like most families, wanted everything back to normal—now!

Unfortunately, recovery is a slow and arduous process. Once a family has established a way of life—even a negative one—change is difficult. For the addictive family, change will require communication about things you may have promised yourself never to talk about. You may have to tell your ten-year-old daughter that you were the one who stole her money so you could go drinking; tell your wife the reason you couldn't be sexual wasn't her fault as you've told her for years, but because you were too high to get aroused; and tell your son you were the one who broke his bike when you knocked it over in the garage. This will require honesty and communication.

The family needs to take time for the members to focus on themselves and learn the skill of personal examination. During active addiction, personal examination and accepting responsibility were dangerous activities with everyone looking for someone to blame. However, personal examination, accountability, and honesty are essential for recovery. We must examine not only how we betrayed family, self, community, and friends, but also how we betrayed the Divine, our Higher Power, and spiritual principles.

In early recovery, the family is still divided. Members quickly become defensive under any signs of stress. Communication still occurs mainly in monologues; dialogue seems too scary. Shame levels are so high that conversations easily slip back into the deadly game of assigning blame. Again, this is why tolerance and patience are needed. It's a slow and gradual process that the recovering family must undergo: Subgroups must disband and the family needs to reunite and become vulnerable as trust develops once again. Disagreement about past events and issues may abound. You may still think your wife paid too much for that dress she bought ten years ago; she still doesn't agree that three TVs are needed in a house with only four people. The perspectives of the addict and co-addict can be quite different. Family members at this stage don't have a long-term vision of what recovery will mean. People still err in the direction of short-term stability instead of long-term mutual growth.

Though necessary, parallel recovery—which allows family members to work on their individual recovery—is only partial recovery. The family gathered around the TV will still experience distance and silence and difficult questions: "What do I say? How do I say I'm sorry and mean it when they've heard me say it a thousand times before? Does Dad feel bad about stealing my money to get drunk? Will he give me the money back? Does he even remember it? How do I talk about the past, my resentments and regrets?"

If family members remain in this "quiet desperation" year after year, then they are settling for only partial recovery. Such a family has found a way to stop the destructive aspects caused by the addiction but has not found a way to re-create a shared value system. The ugliness of active addiction has ceased, and so have the drunken fights, nasty confrontations, and shouting matches. However, the distance between family members—the sad looks across the room—hasn't closed up. A family can and should expect much more from recovery than this.

## The Task of Early Recovery

Recovery requires more than quitting drinking or drug use; it also calls for reestablishing a life of meaning. Instead of choosing friends based on who smokes the best dope, the recovering addict now needs to seek genuine friendships based on respect and support. Recovery involves repositioning oneself in the world.

Each family member must now learn how to live more in accord with one's drive for meaning. The addictive family, on entering recovery, is still driven by instinctual drives of power and pleasure. In treatment and recovery programs, the family must learn to move away from the drives for power and pleasure and toward the drive for meaning. This movement creates the *phenomenon of release*. When we psychologically and spiritually move away from the addictive instincts to use and behave in self-destructive ways and toward value and principles, we are released from self-centeredness and the impulsiveness of an inflated ego. We figuratively walk away from ego toward spiritual principles and meaning. To do this, we first believe in principles of betterment—that honesty will help more than hurt; that humility doesn't mean weakness but strength, and that these and other principles, when put into action, can restore and renew us. When the addict sits and speaks honestly for the first time about her drug history in treatment, or in an AA or NA group, she feels uplifted by a new sense of freedom. Being released from the need to defend the insanity of an addictive life is exhilarating. Other emotions, such as hurt, frustration, and fear, will also seek release.

Recovery is about reentering and reestablishing a life based on spiritual principles and values. Recovery is a spiritual process that reconnects us with the principled parts of our beings and the Divine that lives inside of us. In making this connection, we feel safe and can develop conscious contact with a Higher Power. Let Sandra describe it:

> When I was using, I would go out and get high. Everything was about me. When I used crack, I could see my family, my boys, but I couldn't feel them. Six weeks into recovery, I remember sitting

across from Nate, my five-year-old. I noticed how beautiful his smile was. I had never seen his smile before, not like that. I started to tear up. Now I could feel him smiling deep inside me. Part of me that had been dead for ten years was waking up. I thought, "God, I don't really know him; I've been high his whole life." I went over and picked him up, held and rocked him. I stared into his eyes and told him how beautiful he was. God, how I wanted to be his mother. God, how ashamed I feel. Thank God that I had a wonderful sponsor to help guide me through the emotions of that time.

Sandra is talking about an experience of reconnecting and experiencing life again from her drive for meaning. She was giving birth to herself and to being a mother again. Being released from her ego was both beautiful and painful. Spiritual experiences, like Sandra's, are often experiences of bliss and anguish rolled into a new perspective. The shame and pain Sandra felt resulted from years of betraying her own self-worth and value of being a mother. Her recovery group suggested that Sandra get a locket and put a picture of her boys on one side of the locket and the words *Go to a meeting* on the other side. I saw Sandra five years later with the locket still around her neck.

## Leap of Faith

Recovery requires a leap of faith. Actually, hundreds of leaps. The hardest part about making these leaps is that they involve leaving what you know for the unknown. The practicing addict knows the relief of the high, although he also knows it is destroying him. His spouse knows her resentments. She does not expect her husband to acknowledge or even remember her birthday. The children know not to depend on their parents, and they know how to use their parents' shame to get what they want. This has become the addicted family's world. It may not be the best of worlds, but it is theirs. This family is like a gang fighting to protect turf, not because anyone actually believes in it but because it is all they know. Family members might know that a larger world exists out there, but no one knows how to get themselves out there.

Fundamentally, the family doesn't know how to live a life that is not centered around addiction; how to trust, be honest, and share hurts and truths without getting defensive. The family will need to blindly leap and trust others: Counselors, sponsors, friends, pastors, ministers, and members of their support groups can teach and guide them as they learn new communication skills. It is important to learn how not to hide and be mute when someone says something hurtful; to admit when you're wrong; to call a sponsor when you feel like drinking or getting high. The recovering family must trust again in the human community and in each other. This process requires patience and tolerance by all.

When we take a leap of faith, everything inside of us shakes. Questions, doubts, emotions, and fears rise up. This is natural. Because the addictive family has long been crisis-centered, living without a crisis in the early stage of recovery can be scary. I recall the words of Donald, a teenager I worked with many years ago:

> It had been about a month and there had been no big fights. We were still in treatment. Not one glass had been thrown against the wall. Dad hadn't passed out on the living room floor; all of us just kept going to those meetings. I even caught Mom

whispering one day. All this peace and niceness was spooky; I just couldn't take it anymore. I kept waiting for the other shoe to drop. I liked what was happening, but with each new "nice day" I got tenser inside. So one day I just picked up a glass and threw it against the wall [something that had been a common occurrence in this family], yelled at Dad that he was nothing but a drunk, and ran out of the house. I was expecting to have a free evening from those two, but then they did the weirdest thing they had done in years—they came looking for me. When I saw them standing there with concern instead of anger, I just couldn't take it. I broke down and cried for the first time in years.

After Donald shared this story in the group, the rest of the evening was spent with other families talking about how scary recovery was for them. Most felt like immigrants standing on the shores of a new land.

## Listening to Others' Stories and Telling Our Own

Stories teach. They teach about human limits and spiritual limitlessness. In this early stage of recovery, the recovering family needs to sit in healing circles—whether they be in treatment, Al-Anon, AA, NA, GA, Gam-Anon—and listen to the stories of other addictive families. The family needs to hear how not one family has been able to wish the illness of addiction away. The stories show how we are all connected. We hear how being dependent on spiritual principles and practices can heal us, while being dependent on drugs, alcohol, or other objects and events can destroy us. We start to see that we are each a part of a larger whole. "We are never more than co-authors of our own stories," writes Alasdair MacIntyre in *After Virtue*.

In most treatment centers, groups are used to support people as they tell their personal stories of addiction. Group members sit in a circle so each person can be seen and involved. In the circle, there is no place to hide, unless you do it inside yourself. In listening to the experiences and stories of others, we recognize how we all are each fools and sages. In our recovery groups and circles, we learn that we *are* alone and we *are not* alone; that we are capable of cruelty and capable of being agents of grace; that we have within us a place that is ugly and a place that is holy where love can be created. I first heard of the "healing circles" from a man named Ed:

> I love sitting in the healing circles. I realize that much of my life I've listened very little. It was in the healing circles that I started to listen and learn about life and myself. To me, it's a form of meditation. In listening to the struggles, successes, and stories of others, I found myself. Within these circles, I feel grace and am touched by grace. This is what heals me.

Ed is talking not only about the essence of the recovery group but also about the primary spiritual principles in the first stage of recovery: tolerance and honesty.

## The Collapse

One of the hardest things for family members in early recovery to do is let themselves and their family "collapse." I use the term *collapse* because of how it feels for families to let go of the past and begin rebuilding. It's terrifying and extremely difficult. Remember, families in recovery have organized their lives around the addictive process for many years. Through rationalization, they have justified their addictive system for decades. Emotional reactions also develop to support the addiction. Long-standing behavioral routines and rituals allow family members to live comfortably in denial. The family creates internal and external triggers that push the addict into getting high and the family into controlling behavior. For recovery to be successful, this way of life needs to collapse or end. In this way, psychological room is made for a new way of life. Vickie described the quiet collapse of her marriage:

> During those first couple of years, all we did was fall apart, but not in big dramatic ways, which was our old style. In the past, everything, and I mean everything, had been centered on Pete's drinking and drug use, and now with that out of the way, we truly didn't know how to be with each other. I caught Pete staring at me one day. I asked him what he was staring at. He replied, "My wife, and I have no idea what to do with her." He was right. These little moments of honesty were what we came to call our breakdown moments. You could feel pieces of the old way of life falling aside like pieces of a glacier breaking into the sea to be carried away. During those first years, we had no idea what to do with each other. Many nights no one spoke. We were in limbo, between two worlds. We couldn't go back, but didn't know how to go forward.

Vickie's family, like most recovering families, had many old thoughts, attitudes, and behaviors to let go of in order to make room for the new. The old addictive system says survival is based on control and how well you can defend yourself. The new system says survival depends on letting go and on how well you bring principles, support, and community into your life. The old system says keep an eye on your addict. The new system says let go of your addict— you can't control him anyway.

Allowing the family to collapse may be compared to blowing up your own house when you don't know where you will live. For many families, the dismantling process is like taking down an old structure, brick by brick, board by board. For a time it feels as if you are being asked to walk backward through life. Patsy, a fifteen-year-old, spoke of her terror in family group:

> Ever since I can remember, I've been my mother's mother. I've looked after her for years. I would clean her up and get her to bed when she would come home and get sick after an evening of drinking. That is, *if* she came home. Friday nights have become my evening to sit and wait for her and pray for her safe return. I can't remember a Friday night I've gone out with friends. Hell, I can't remember having friends. Everything was centered on caring for Mom. Now you tell me to let go and focus on my own life. What life? She has been my life for as long as I can remember. If I don't look out for her, who will? And what am I to do? Just walk into the cafeteria at school and say, "Okay everybody, I'm ready to have friends now." I hate that phrase "let go." You say it so easily. Do you have any idea of what you are asking?

It isn't just addicts who need to let their world collapse, but co-addicts, like Patsy, as well. Patsy's personality and identity were defined by how well she cared for her addicted mother. Recovery challenged her. She didn't know what to do:

> I'm so scared of what you're asking me to do. I have no idea how to be fifteen. Don't you think I would like to sit with a bunch of girlfriends and talk about the boys in our class? I notice them, you know. I wouldn't know what to say or do. I'm not ashamed of what I've done. I did what had to be done—someone had to look after her. I'm just ashamed that I don't know how to be me now.

In this group, the kids from other families offered Patsy what only they could offer—they could begin teaching her how to be fifteen. They started by having an overnight slumber party in her honor. Patsy's first response was to look over at her mother, who reassured her that she would be okay. In one of her first genuine acts of mothering in years, she said to Patsy: "I'll go to an extra meeting that night and ask my sponsor if I can sleep at her house, so you don't have to worry about me. I'm sorry. I can't give you your childhood back, but they can—go be with them."

## Reaching Out

In early recovery, the addictive family must reach outside of itself for help. Members need to go to aftercare and support meetings; read recovery literature; get a sponsor; attend counseling, recovery meetings, and religious services, if that is important to the family. How well family members do in recovery is partially determined by how much support they seek and receive. If we had heart disease, we'd welcome the help of the community. If we had cancer, we would contact doctors, nurses, cancer support groups, and information centers to help us heal. It's the same with addiction: We need our community to heal.

The addictive family cannot teach itself how to fully

recover. Members may know addiction, but they do not yet know recovery. They need to let themselves become dependent for a time on those who do. The addict who feels like getting high needs to call and talk to a recovery friend, or go to a support meeting. The parent who is shaking inside because her newly recovering adolescent son has decided to attend a school dance where there might be drugs needs to call a recovery friend or attend an Al-Anon meeting. In recovery, we don't need to be alone anymore.

## Borrowing a Value System

A major task in early recovery is finding and attaching to a support system. The Twelve Step groups of Alcoholics Anonymous, Al-Anon, Ala-teen, Narcotics Anonymous, Gamblers Anonymous, Gam-Anon, and the other types of support group like Rational Recovery, Women for Sobriety, and Couples Anonymous are places where addicts and family members can learn how to live a new way of life. Families will need to attach themselves to the knowledge, skills, and values of those who have gone before them, so they can heal from this physical and spiritual illness.

Some recovery slogans address this issue of borrowing values. The first is "Act as if"; the second, "Fake it till you make it." These slogans acknowledge that you may not know how to do some things right now, but you can act as if you do, and then eventually you will know how. This is not pretending, but hoping and believing. Maybe you've been yelling and putting people down for years. Now, you can act as if you like people, and in a short time this act may be the truth. Besides, yelling and anger were just defense systems. Maybe you believe you have nothing to say because your drunken husband has told you that for years. Now, you can act as if you have worthwhile ideas and speak at your meeting. Eventually, you'll find your voice. These are examples of borrowing the values of the group until you can integrate them into your way of life.

A value system is a collection of principles, such as honesty, respect, patience, fellowship, service work, listening, and willingness to help others. When people first enter recovery, they may be unclear on what they truly value and what they want to value. For this reason, new members in recovery support groups are encouraged to take on the group's collective value system as they reevaluate and rebuild their own. This allows family members to compare their lack of values from living in an addictive family to that of others in recovery. They can see how they might have been in the right ballpark, but just playing the wrong game. They are encouraged to examine how the illness of addiction has distorted and attacked their value system. Adopting a new value system can help transform individuals and families. Listen to Ned describe his transformation:

> For over ten years I acted in a disrespectful way toward my family and friends. I didn't care about anyone else—all I cared about was me. I took illegal drugs. I yelled at and abused my family and my friends. I stole and had no respect for others or their property. Being in this group taught me how to act. I was given a sponsor who started to teach me right from wrong and how to act respectful. At first, it was an act. I "acted as if," *as if* I knew how to be respectful. If I yelled at someone, I had to go apologize, even if I felt they had it coming. I had to do service work and do small regular acts of respect. Eventually this value system I had borrowed

transformed me. Just like drugs had the power to transform me, these new behaviors, attitudes, and principles also had powers to transform me. I became a respectful and respectable person.

In early recovery, it is important that all family members, not just the addicts, participate in a recovery program. It helps to quicken the recovery process. The common language, rituals, and messages of hope help the family build common, spiritual ground.

## Spiritual Principles Most Helpful in Early Recovery

When a person enters recovery and borrows from this new value system, she will find some spiritual principles more important at certain times than others. When one begins to build a new house, certain skills—design, excavation, and the placement of concrete footings—are needed when preparing a foundation. Plumbing and electrical work will not be needed until later in the process. Recovery is similar to building a house in that it calls on different spiritual principles and skills at different times. Following are three primary and essential principles needed in the first stage of recovery: honesty, fellowship, and surrender.

### Honesty

Honesty, the first spiritual principle, has enormous healing power. An addicted mother must first become honest with herself about her use to see the need for outside help. When the alcoholic admits he lost his job due to his drinking and not because his employer had it out for him, he opens up to seeking advice and guidance. When the adolescent admits that she sticks a needle in her arm because she is addicted and not because she had a poor childhood, she realizes the need for a new way of life.

Honesty not only helps define the problem but also provides a solution by enabling the person to see that recovery demands help from other people. When addicts and co-addicts become honest about their loss of control, they realize the need for help from professionals and others. Honesty will be needed throughout recovery. But without it in the first stage, there is no hope.

### Fellowship

The spiritual principle of fellowship is also critical in early recovery. Addiction is based on ego and selfishness— these are not principles one can live by. The illness of addiction isolates family members not only from each other but also from resources that will heal them. The fellowship that is found in recovery is based on a *we* or a community of sufferers who are healing and enjoying a new sobriety and freedom.

In the land of *me*, the only relationship that counts is the one with yourself. In the land of *we*, on the other hand, relationship with others takes on great importance. Being part of a community challenges us to listen, offer support to others, negotiate instead of manipulate, and see that helping others, not controlling them, enriches us. When we learn how to be part of a fellowship, we learn much about how to be a part of a family.

The principle of fellowship works to break down the addictive self-centeredness and allows individuals to connect with activities, principles, and healthy people. Selfishness and the accompanying isolation are often confronted in a recovery group. In the fellowship of meetings and after-meeting gatherings, the craving addict learns to call a sponsor or group member and stay connected when the urge to use or drink occurs. The teenager in Alateen, ready to act out his anger against the family, can call a sponsor or attend a group meeting to talk and listen, instead of reacting. The *we*, or fellowship, in recovery offers a healthy alternative to the individual still stinging from years of living in an addictive family system. Patrick explains how the fellowships saved him from relapsing:

> I would go for two or three months and then the craving would return. I believed I had to do it on my own. I was so ashamed of my past that I guess I didn't believe I was entitled to help. I remember when that changed. I was getting ready to walk out the door and go to my dealer's house when the face of one of the guys in my group came to mind. He had said to call at any time if needed. At first I tried to forget him. But for some reason, I called him. He was glad I had called and told me not to leave until he got there. He wouldn't let me out of his sight for days. We stayed up talking until two or three in the morning, working out the issues and shame of the past. What he did best was listen, which kept me talking. He is my sponsor to this day. "We are in this together," he said. "I need you sober and you need me sober."

### Surrender

Surrender is also vital to early recovery. When we surrender, we admit to complete defeat. Everything inside of us may say, "No, I can lick this disease on my own." Still, we must learn to admit that we have lost control of ourselves and that we are powerless to stop the addiction ruining our families and us. We must learn that we can't control the addicts in our families. We have tried in the past, and it did not work.

Much of life is about surrender. It liberates us from destructive behavior, thoughts, and attitudes. You engage in an argument with your spouse. You know your spouse is wrong, and you have something at your office to prove it. Do you drive to your office, an hour away, to get it? In recovery, it is hoped you will hear the small, quiet voice speaking to you: "Is it really worth it? It's Friday night; do you want to be driving that far to prove a point?" When we surrender, we give up the argument, the need to be right, and focus more on what is truly important—the relationship. Once you let go, you may find your spouse acknowledging your position or belief. Perhaps it was only the tone you used that put your spouse in a defensive position. When you surrender and let your tone change, your spouse can change position without feeling forced to submit to your will.

The paradox of recovery is that when we admit complete defeat, we become victorious. Surrender and the admission of hopelessness always bring help. Strangely, it is hard for family members to admit that their love, hard work, and dedication alone could not heal addiction.

## Relapse Issues

What families in recovery fear most is the addict's relapse. The fear is not unreasonable. Many addicts will relapse early on in their recovery. This is part of the illness. Relapse is *not* about the family, even if the addict says it is. Often the addict in relapse returns to her old behavior and blames others as a defense. Harry, twenty-five, frequently relapsed and blamed his mother for his slips until she went into treatment for herself—without Harry:

I always blamed my mother for my slips. "If only

you had helped me like I asked you to, I wouldn't have had to return to my using friends. If only you would show a little understanding about what I'm trying to do! It's not easy to try to recover and work at the same time. You should help me financially to get my feet back on the ground." This worked until Mom went to family treatment. Afterward, when I went over to her house drunk and she opened the door and saw me, she told me I wasn't welcome at her house anymore in that condition. I told her to give me twenty dollars and I would go away. She said the only money she'd give is to pay for a taxi to take me to detox. I said no, and she shut the door. I stood in the middle of the lawn, whining and hollering. I got that ride to detox because she called the police. Boy was I mad and scared! Something had changed.

Harry continued to drink and slip for a couple more years, but he started to have a more honest and respectful relationship with his mother. He would see her only when he was sober, and she quit putting him down when he did relapse. She had accepted his relapses as part of the illness, but she did continue to expect him to get and stay sober.

The addict isn't the only one in a family who can relapse. Every family member can relapse, not by using alcohol or drugs but by returning to old behavior, resentments, anger, unwillingness to listen, and controlling behavior. Almost everyone in the family will probably experience some relapse. Harry's mother had been relapsing, too, by enabling her son and giving him money.

Family members may find it difficult to get back on track because they don't have a specific behavior like using drugs or alcohol to identify their relapses. They will often need the help of their group or sponsor to observe their old behavior.

## Shift from Other-Examination to Self-Examination

One of the major shifts that needs to occur in early recovery is from examining the behavior of others to examining one's own behavior. In the addictive family system, a peculiar rule is applied to all family members: I will examine your behavior, you examine mine, but never do we examine our own.

In the addictive system, family members are looking over their shoulders and watching others. "Don't tell me what I did wrong; who are you to talk?" "Yes, I did that but what about you?" "Oh yeah! When are you going to listen to me?" "I'm just telling you this for your own good!" In this dysfunctional family, admitting personal wrongdoing and taking responsibility for your own behavior would be like painting a bull's-eye on your chest.

Recovery requires that we learn to focus on the things we can change—ourselves. In taking an inventory of our own behavior, rather than the other person's behavior, a new type of struggle gets set up. Slowly, over time, integrity struggles instead of power struggles develop. In healthy families, members regularly examine how they are part of the problem and how they can contribute to the solution. This challenges and encourages everyone to do the same. This is how the true meaning and nature of any problem can be discovered.

The only way to dismantle our own defense system is to take responsibility for it, examine it, and then work to change it. This is why recovery involves lots of inventorying and examining of why we betrayed our spiritual principles. This was a big hurdle for Jeremy to get past in his treatment:

I wanted to focus on my upbringing while in treatment. One day, out of frustration, I yelled at my counselor, "Don't you care a bit about what I had to put up with as a child?" She said, "Only if it will keep you sober, but you seem to use it to get loaded." She was right, but I was so afraid of looking at myself—I knew what was back there, I knew what made the shadows on the walls, and I didn't want to go there. I had hurt people during my addiction and wanted instead to focus on how they had hurt me. She was a good counselor; she taught me how to focus on what I could change—me. But boy did she pay a price! I was mean to her. I worked hard trying to get myself kicked out of treatment. You know what changed it around? I was watching out the window one afternoon and saw my mean old counselor walking with her arm around her daughter, who had come to pick her up. The looks on their faces showed great joy. I realized she was just trying to put her arm around me, and I was afraid.

Jeremy began to accept responsibility for his own actions. It isn't easy when you have been blaming others for years. All family members in recovery must stop fault-finding and begin fault-admitting, stop other-examination and begin self-examination. The spouse must learn to say, "You know, I believe we had a bad night last night because I came home grumpy and took it out on you." The parent might say: "I could have listened better and heard that you were scared about passing your test. If I had heard your fears, I might have helped you study or review for the test. I'll try to listen better and hear what you're really saying." This is what it means to be a healthy family.

# Summary of Phase 1

## EARLY RECOVERY

| | |
|---|---|
| **Tasks:** | Admit and accept addiction as an illness. |
| | Change from seeing who is wrong to what is wrong. |
| | Build personal responsibility for how addiction has been dealt with in the family. |
| | Build outside systems that support recovery. |
| | Learn to reach outside of self for help in solving and discussing issues and problems. |
| **Changes in Family Interaction Patterns:** | A collapse of the old system of interaction within the family. |
| | The family is involved in parallel recovery with each member working at connecting and developing an individual support system. The family is still mainly divided. |
| | The family is still operating with short-term focus. The future remains very scary. |
| | The family practices listening, but it is a hit-and-miss event. |
| | Longer and longer periods of communication occur without defense reactions. |
| **Other Characteristics:** | Communication is still mainly monologues, but attempts are being made to establish dialogue. |
| | Blame is still used. |
| | There's disagreement over the past and who's at fault. |

Fig. 14

# CHAPTER 9

# MIDDLE RECOVERY: UNDERSTANDING AND ACCEPTANCE

During middle recovery, the family is consciously experiencing some of the benefits of recovery. The addict has some sobriety; communication has improved; family members are beginning to trust that the peace and quiet at home will not be shattered. Fear lessens and hope gradually returns. The tree that had been uprooted by addiction and now replanted in recovery is taking root. The transition of early recovery is over and good habits are taking hold. Family life is becoming more reliable, consistent, and happier. Instinct and ego are being replaced by principles of betterment and a supportive community.

The family—not just the addict—is beginning to understand and accept the nature of addiction and how it has affected all members of the family. Spouses understand why they, too, need a regular support group, such as

Al-Anon or Gam-Anon. As members understand how each one in the family has been hurt by addiction, blaming stops. Family members see the genuine remorse of the addict, who now tries to communicate respectfully.

When family members see each other investing in recovery, going to their meetings, reading meditation books, preparing notes on a Step to share with their group, hope gets created. At this stage, the family is still watchful of the addict to see how invested he is in staying sober; however, members feel more accepting. Some of the wounds of the past are healing but not entirely. Some are forgiven; others are not. Family members are more capable of accepting other's opinions. Now the family works more conscientiously to create a system based on meaning instead of power and pleasure.

The understanding and knowledge that comes from a firm commitment to recovery starts to heal the family. This is a time when the family's true goal becomes intimacy and renewed love. Family members attend recovery meetings; they don't hide their recovery from each other. Through a better understanding of the fragility of the human condition, everyone works to be kinder and more courteous. Family members start to see and feel their true importance. Egos deflate and self-esteem rises.

The addictive system of the past promised quick solutions and better days ahead. The family now invests little in these get-happy-quick schemes. Thus, members slowly learn to be positive. They may say "thank you" after a nice meal; children look for their father after school to let him know they're home; the couple seek private time for themselves. Maybe a husband gives his wife a card for no reason other than to express his appreciation. Simple pleasures become important again. Family interactions show a deeper understanding of each other. Pleasure as a goal is seen as suspect, so the family focuses more on things like being kind to each other, showing consideration, and expressing genuine concern. Siblings call when they are going to be late. Getting even becomes less and less important. All know that trust and respect must now be earned, not demanded.

In this stage of recovery, many marriages either break apart or grow more solid. Marriages and families may now require outside help. There seem to be two times in recovery when marriages are most vulnerable. The first occurs within the first year of recovery. All hope for the marriage may have left years before, but now that the addict is sober, the co-addict, believing he is free from obligations, exits the marriage. The second time occurs during this middle stage of recovery. At this point, a couple either find new ways to connect and reestablish a meaningful and enriching life together or discover that the marriage has been damaged beyond repair. The couple may have just grown too far apart over the years.

## Major Characteristics of This Time

Through understanding and acceptance of the illness of addiction, the family has healed enough that its members have developed a new vision. A son may see his parents in the football stands cheering, and Dad is sober. A wife considers buying a gift or surprising her husband for their anniversary instead of wondering if she should call the lawyer.

This new vision of the family as a place of enjoyment and comfort, possibilities and hope, is an eventful shift. Family members still fear becoming too vulnerable, but the personal successes they are experiencing have an accumulative effect.

Success breeds hope. The longer individuals work their programs, the longer the addict stays sober, the more the family believes that a new way of life is possible, the more benefits come to the family. Kids start to believe Dad will stay sober. Brothers and sisters are glad to attend their brother's treatment sessions. The knowledge they gain in treatment is now improving their lives.

At this point, spiritual principles are put into action often. The family begins operating again from its drive for meaning. With addiction in remission, the addict and her family can again believe in and practice spiritual principles in all aspects of their lives. Their continued involvement in their recovery group or support group deepens their understanding and acceptance of how spiritual principles heal.

When his father started getting honest, Jimmy was amazed at his own understanding and at how accepting his father was:

> My father was a couple of years sober, but I had given up on him. He had lied to me all my life. He said he would show up for this or that and never would. He was sitting on the couch looking upset. He asked me if I would come sit with him. He would not look directly at me, said he was too ashamed, but he started talking. He was in pain. He said his sponsor was having him look at what an irresponsible father he had been during his drinking and early recovery, and it was becoming clear to him how much damage he had done. He then described two different incidents that had happened three or four years ago. We had never spoken of these incidents. His recall of the details and the accuracy of how he had hurt me took me back. The details of what he was saying showed me

that he was seeing things clearly and was being honest. Also, he was thinking how I had been affected and not just thinking about himself. Strangely, I hated him at that moment. Why was he doing this? How dare he act in a way that created hope? It wasn't fair! His words were destroying my sanctuary. He said he wouldn't say he was sorry and ask me to forgive him, because that would be unfair to me, but he would try and earn my forgiveness.

Jimmy's father was starting to act like a dad again. Now, Jimmy is struggling to decide whether he wants a father. Should he give his father a second chance? If he does, how does he open his heart after keeping it closed all these years? These are the types of questions that arise in middle recovery.

## More Spirituality and Family Stability

Now that all the family members are practicing spiritual principles, their relationship with time changes. They are not so obsessed and controlling about the moment at hand. More accepting and trusting, they believe more in their future and are less haunted by the past. They are able to forgo the instinctual gratification of power and pleasure for more meaningful pursuits.

In addiction, the family lives more by instinct than by spirit. The focus is on immediate satisfaction and runs against the grain of spiritual principles such as restraint, delayed gratification, patience, hope for the future, and meaning. When we live within the realm of instinct, we live restrained by time. We are like a squirrel that instinctually knows winter is coming. We gather more; we seek more. The addict increasingly seeks more sensations of the high. The family increasingly seeks more sensations of control.

In middle recovery, as individuals and families, we turn away from our instinctual side toward a more spiritual life. Upon reaching a certain level of stability, members of the family will start to risk again. Maybe your brother now tells you he is angry at you for wearing his shirt. This may not seem too important at first, but the brother hasn't confronted you for three years in fear that you might get high and he would be to blame. Maybe Dad asks to attend a father-daughter dinner at church and you agree. Again, this request might appear minor, but it isn't when you consider that two years ago you lifted your father's head out of his soup bowl so he wouldn't drown when he passed out from mixing alcohol and sleeping pills.

Families now begin to believe in meaning and seek intimacy and connection with others. In middle recovery, the concrete has dried enough to support the entire family and the weight of different relationships. Communication is deepening. People work to listen and not just to be heard.

In the active addictive family, the future is scary because it seems unpredictable and full of more pain, fights, disrespect, and danger. In middle recovery, the family becomes increasingly stable, as it now focuses on spiritual principles, which are more promising. Karen, an old-timer in recovery, spoke about this:

> The calendar had become my enemy. I looked at it and would think, "How long can I hang on?" The pain was bad. I could see my addiction on the faces of my kids. There was the calendar saying that the beginning of the holidays was a month away. I went into a depression. What was I going to do?

And the money! Where was I going to get the money for presents and for my drugs? I went crazy. I took all the calendars in the house, threw them in the fireplace, and told the kids that from now on we were living one day at a time. No more holidays, no more birthdays, no more Mother's Day. They were to expect nothing from me. My son just shook his head, said they already didn't, and walked away. It took us eight years into recovery before we could enjoy the holidays again. That first sober Thanksgiving, only one of the kids came. Last year they all came and brought their families. It was great.

Karen is now a wonderful example of the spirit of the holidays. She doesn't fear the future as much anymore. It's not a constant reminder of more bad things to come. The slogan "One day at a time" holds a new meaning for Karen today; it helps her focus on recovery, build confidence, and realize that tomorrow will bring more of the peace and recovery she enjoys in her life today.

## From Borrowed Values to Integrated Values

In early recovery, the addict and family borrow the principles and values of recovery and try them on to see if they can fit their lives. They act "as if" they will, though they may not even believe in the principles. But now, after experiencing the authentic power of the principles of betterment, family members bring them more and more into their lives. The family now understands a need for values and the need to work a recovery program. In their work and personal lives, family members are becoming more comfortable and skilled in applying spiritual values, such as honesty, understanding, and acceptance, to their daily lives. With continued practice, the principles become skills for each family member.

These spiritual principles bring comfort to family members. Parents see their kids not backing away, but coming closer when they are treated with respect. Kids see enthusiasm and interest from their parents, as the children learn to speak in honest and respectful ways again. Children smile as Mom tries hard to listen instead of lecturing.

Family members are developing a "conscious contact" with these principles—if they quiet themselves and listen, they can hear these principles guiding them to a better life. Gerald spoke of the "classroom" of principles in his head:

> Most often, and always during my addiction, my mind is like a disruptive classroom. Everyone is doing something different, and everyone is jockeying for attention. In recovery, I learned that there is a teacher in this classroom, and if I sit quietly at my desk and focus my attention at the front of the room, I can see the teacher writing on the board, speaking in a steady but soft voice. If I listen, I get interested, and best of all I learn. I guess that is what they mean by conscious contact.

As we learn the lessons of recovery, we put principles into action and create meaning with others. Simple as it may sound, recovery is about being safe to be around again. By middle recovery, individuals are starting to integrate spiritual principles like integrity, loyalty, humility, openness, and acceptance into their beings.

## Spiritual Principles Most Helpful in Middle Recovery

During middle recovery, a time of regeneration and faster-paced growth, certain spiritual principles are especially important. They are accountability, humility, gratitude, and discipline

### Accountability

A very powerful principle, accountability means we become responsible for our relationships and spiritual principles. During active addiction, the addict of the family worked hard to get others to be accountable. "It's not my fault that I drink. All you do is criticize me." "It's not my fault that I question you. You're untrustworthy." Recovery demands that we become accountable for ourselves. Much of the work of recovery, especially during middle recovery, involves taking inventory of our own behavior and self-reflection. This helps us become more focused on our own behavior, feelings, and thoughts—not in a selfish way, but in a way that makes us more account-able to others. In the end, accountability gives us *more* not *less* freedom. When we were practicing addicts, we believed we were free spirits, accountable to no one or nothing. However, the truth is that we were accountable to and sickly dependent on alcohol or other drugs. We were far from being free. In true accountability, we take responsibility for our own behavior and gain the opportunity to change. Now that we regularly show up to our recovery meetings, do our readings, put in our eight hours on the job, we know a new happiness and freedom.

### Humility

The basic ingredient of humility is a desire to place that which is spiritual before ego. It is building character before comfort. If someone calls during supper and needs help, you let your meal get cold as you listen and encourage the person's sobriety. In humility, we step away from our inflated egos and create and find meaning in things and people outside of our narrow worlds. When our kids give us a great chance to lecture them, our egos may drool at the opportunity, but instead we now listen and encourage them to share more with us. This attracts our children to us. When they aren't constantly afraid of our lecturing them, children will seek our companionship and support. If your child is having school problems, instead of yelling and lecturing him to do better and try harder, you might go to school with him, talk with his teachers, and set up a homework schedule for him.

As we step away from our inflated egos, we learn that we can control very little. Humility lets us see our correct size—we're neither giants nor dwarfs, impeccably wonderful or pitifully bad. Humility transforms our self-centeredness, self-will, and desire to control things and people into a desire to fit in, not stand out. We get to the parade early and get a good seat on the curb instead of complaining that we are not the grand marshal or on a float. Now we see self-centeredness as a weakness that humility can transform into a strength.

### Gratitude

In middle recovery, gratitude becomes more central in our lives. Because we can now see the differences between a sober life and one centered around drinking and drugging, we feel genuinely happy to be free of addiction. We understand just how deadly and damaging the illness of addiction is. We see how meaningless life had become and feel our lives regaining purpose and meaning. Now we can appreciate simple pleasures such as playing with our three-year-old granddaughter, sitting on the front porch, bicycling down a street, or receiving a compliment.

Gratitude heals. It reminds us that our essence, or core, is good and sufficient. Gratitude works against the impulse for accumulating more and instead concentrates on accepting what is. The more gratitude we have, the less attention, drugs, control, or money we desire. We are enough. This day, this hour, is enough. I was taught a lot about gratitude by a very young man I once knew named Kevin. He had contracted AIDS from injecting heroin:

> Most of the people in the NA groups I go to are fighting for their lives. But you know I'm truly grateful, even with AIDS. I had been in treatment four times before and never took it seriously. Now for the last couple of years, I've taken my recovery seriously and finally gotten to live a good life. I don't get to choose if I'll live or die. My addiction has already made that choice for me. But I do get to choose whether I die with dignity or without. I pray each day for help in working a good recovery program. You see, my death depends on it.

Kevin died six months later, with much gratitude and dignity. He died sober and with family and friends surrounding him.

### Discipline

Once again discipline is the ability to stay consistently connected to spiritual principles. We need discipline in middle recovery to develop effective recovery rituals and routines. Sitting down each morning as a family or as an individual, taking ten minutes to read a meditation, or attending an AA or Al-Anon meeting can create a routine and establish lifelong friendships. Regular discipline allows one to stay attached to spiritual principles for longer and longer periods. Discipline can help us control our impulses, which may give us the few extra minutes we need to help prevent a slip or relapse. Discipline in recovery requires us regularly to surrender our egos over to that which is best for us. It may mean going to an Al-Anon meeting even though we're feeling tired or sorry for ourselves. Remember, authentic power comes from making choices that are in our best interest. Spiritual discipline leads to an increase in ethical, authentic power and a decrease in the need for false or pseudo-power.

## Safety Causes Surprises

As the family and its members are led increasingly by their drives for meaning instead of power or pleasure, spiritual by-products are created. One of these by-products is safety. Because family members are less reactive, harsh, and aggressive, everyone feels more safe to be vulnerable and admit to their own feelings. Issues that were shelved long ago can now be taken out and addressed in a safe environment. Perhaps a son, who now feels comfortable around his father, with four years of sobriety, finds himself repeatedly dreaming about his father chasing and screaming at him, something the father actually did when he was drunk. The son's current feelings of safety allow the issue to resurface. It may now be safe for deeper wounds to be resolved. Some part of the son believes that he and his father are ready to deal with these old wounds.

One of the most dramatic examples of this was with a client named Vincent. Vincent was in his thirties and had grown up in an alcoholic, abusive home. After a couple of months in therapy, Vincent started to flinch when I would move my hand through my hair in a certain way. In time, Vincent remembered that his father used to line up the children, including him, and slap them in the face. At times, he just pretended to slap them. If they flinched, he would laugh and slap them for flinching. Over time, Vincent had learned not to flinch under any conditions. Now, in the safety of his recovery and our therapeutic relationship, this issue was resurfacing, and Vincent's natural reaction to flinch reappeared. For about a month and a half, Vincent reported flinching at certain hand movements. His family was scared by this reaction until Vincent explained it. It was as if the old poisons that had been slapped into him by his father were working their way out. He actually started to feel good that he could flinch again because it meant that he was healing the abuse of his past life.

The gift for working hard in recovery is that you eventually get to work on issues that are more complex. It is like math. Once you learn to add and subtract, you advance to multiplication and division, eventually to algebra, calculus, and so on. Recovery shows this same type of progression. Feeling safe creates a spiritual classroom in which we can learn. We build on each of our lessons, resolving past issues as we move forward.

## Reforming

A family doesn't recover in one day. Creating a new way of life takes effort and time. As fear lessens and trust develops, most family members decide they would like to reconnect as a unit. Not all, but most. From this desire, the family begins reforming.

Small subgroups form. Two brothers may meet on their own for supper every Tuesday night. A daughter may offer to go shopping with her dad, who is now a year and a half sober. Implied in this offer is the subtle message that just maybe Dad is worth trusting again. A son might turn to his parents two years into recovery and state that he'd like to go on vacation with them next year. This is how family members put their toes in to test the recovery water.

These subgroups slowly include other family members. It may take a few years before the family will feel like a family again because emotional wounds from addiction are deep and need time to heal. Heather has etched in her mind the day she and her family began to consider themselves healed:

> I was working outside on the lawn with my husband, Terry. I had been sober a little over three years when my eighteen-year-old daughter, Ruth, came out from the house and stood on the porch. After watching us for a time, she came over and kissed each of us on the cheek. Terry asked her what that was for. She replied, "For all the mistakes and for what you two have done with them." With that she walked back into the house and left Terry and me standing there knowing exactly what she meant. Terry looked at me and smiled. We kissed and went back to cleaning up the yard. That was the day we all re-signed our contract to be a family again.

# Summary of Phase 2

## MIDDLE RECOVERY

| Tasks: | Talk through past hurts and abuses. |
|---|---|
| | Create a new perspective of family that incorporates principles and vision of continued recovery. |
| | Continue and deepen personal responsibility for how one's actions affect all family members. |
| | Continue and deepen the relationship with outside support systems. |
| **Changes in Family Interaction Patterns:** | Returning safety is allowing tougher issues to rise to the surface and seek resolution. |
| | Family members are blending together their parallel recoveries into a family view of recovery. |
| | The family is reforming around principles of betterment and an increased desire and belief in intimacy. Formless love starts to take a new form. |
| | The family is developing a longer-term focus. The future becomes less and less scary. |
| | The family practices active listening. |
| **Other Characteristics:** | There is increased understanding and true knowledge of what the issues of the past were about. |
| | A renewal of spirits starts to take hold. |

Fig. 15

# CHAPTER 10

# LATE RECOVERY:
# LOVE

In late recovery, the tree planted years ago in treatment now bears fruit. Comfort comes regularly. One of my clients came in and bragged that his daughter had come home from school and given him a hug. He asked, "What's that for?" His daughter said that in health class they were studying alcoholism, and she just wanted to thank him for "coming home from that ugly world." In this stage of recovery, the past is past. The power of addiction is still respected, but now that the family members are attending their recovery meetings and working hard to deepen their programs, the dangers of addiction are not immediate. Family members trust each other's recovery and come through for each other by continuing to work solid recovery programs.

## Healing the Past

The wounds of the past are healed. The using years have lost most of their power to attract and the family is nesting in recovery. The children do not feel their insides tighten up when their father arrives home from work. The father doesn't stand outside the door of the house afraid to open it and start another evening of fighting with his drugged-up son. Family members are not held captive by their own instinctual impulses. Parents can be around children who are angry and be supportive instead of becoming angry themselves. Children can see parents upset and not panic. The drives for power and control no longer rule the home; instead family members use self-regulation and weather crises much better. A son, grounded by his parents, may become angry and pick on his sister, but now the parent can calmly intervene and say: "It wasn't your sister who grounded you. If you have an issue, talk to me. Don't pick on her." The parent has learned by now to control herself and then address the problem. The parent has gained respect, not by demanding it but by earning it. The hundreds of meetings the parent has attended and the hours he has spent patiently listening to others are paying off.

The recovering family in this stage now understands that pain and struggles are the raw materials that build intimacy and self-esteem. A sense of purpose returns. Parents get up in the morning and struggle to find the energy to go to work because their children's needs are important. They—not drugs—are the parents' purpose now. Parents understand how important they are to their children. Individuals and family members have grown a *real* sense of importance that replaces the old addictive grandiosity and self-centeredness.

Families now see it is their job to influence others by modeling hope, hard work, peace, excellence, community, and spiritual principles. When the wife is depressed because she didn't get her promotion, her husband now sits, listens, and encourages. In this stage, family members have mostly given up the futility of trying to control each other. They now realize that resentment and resistance occur if you try to control another. Only through positive influence and letting family members control their own lives do you create respect. Making suggestions instead of delivering proclamations can help families relax and regain a sense of purpose.

The recovering addict, through empathy, now realizes and appreciates what his family has endured during the addiction. He knows what it must have felt like for his wife to read a drunkenly scrawled suicide note left on the kitchen table before he disappeared for a weekend binge. Family members understand how their terror caused them to try to control the addict's every move. The family in late recovery works to be of service to others. When the wife sees her husband struggling to get dinner made or the dishes done so he can go out for the evening, she puts the newspaper down and helps. She is no longer afraid that her offer will lead to an argument or a lecture about how little she does.

In these and many other ways, a couple and family learn to love again. Their love, reduced to formlessness in addiction, has found form again. Through tolerance, self-examination, new communication skills, and many hours of talking issues out instead of acting them out, a couple and the family have formed close bonds again, or in some cases developed them for the first time. Care and concern is seen; love is demonstrated daily. Early in this book we discussed the mission of every family: The primary spiritual task of families is to create and sustain love. In late recovery, families return to this primary task. Love is evident in the smiles, laughing, and joking around at the dinner table; in someone listening to another describe her day; in the parents showing up for school conferences (without whiskey on their breath); and in being asked to baby-sit grandchildren whose parents once swore you were the devil. These actions illustrate love put in the motion of everyday life. They are examples of a family creating and sustaining love. Family members may continue to struggle daily with issues, but instead of covering up their imperfections, they now learn from them.

## Mistakes Are Not Met with Overreactions

In active addiction, mistakes—such as misplacing telephone numbers, being ten minutes late from work, and buying the wrong brand of scotch—were attacked and used as excuses to put another person down. Everyone became edgy. Anyone who made mistakes was shamed for them. In early and middle recovery, these attacks mostly end, though mistakes still have the power to spook families in these stages: "Will I get jumped on? Yelled at?" Mistakes in early recovery often open old wounds and dredge up fears that family life is again getting out of control. By late recovery, families see and regularly take their own inventory. This activity is not intended merely to solve a problem, but is now a way of life.

In late recovery, catching others making mistakes has lost most of its power. Because each family member is accountable for his or her own actions, mistakes are not viewed as shameful. Imperfection is allowed. There may be tension, but no panic or sense of doom when a parent says, "I want to talk to you about something you did." Family life becomes simpler.

The family can now sit and spend the evening together just talking, playing cards, and showing each other things they're discovering on the Internet. The real agenda is to connect and catch up on each other's lives. Little things start to impress you again. I loved the way Judy talked and teased her mother:

> She was a bad drunk and boy did I think she was stupid. She's been sober ten years now, and I'm twenty-two. Now I think my mother is smart. Mom asks good questions. Her questions cause you to think and go deeper. My friends love to come and sit with her and just talk. We actually discuss world events. Ten years ago, the house was silent, except when she went into a rage. I guess she was just preserving her brain in alcohol until it was needed.

## Dialogue and Recommitment

Family members now open up to others. They make room for others in their lives instead of filling up the space with their own egos. The monologue of the past pitted ego against ego. Now the dialogue of recovery layers ideas, emotions, and egos in a way that makes room for all. Communication becomes a collaborative experience of shared meaning. When a parent learns he is getting a nice bonus at work, instead of keeping it quiet, he talks about it with his spouse and children at dinner. They talk about spending the bonus for a family vacation. Everyone happily shares ideas on how to spend it. Dialogue helps clarify issues and solve problems. Gone are the days when the addict or co-addict ranted and raved, when no one listened or cared to.

The family has learned to be together and be separate at the same time. The family has learned the importance of placing principles before personalities. A daughter might have sworn she would never forgive her father for being drunk when he came to pick her up at a friend's house. But after years go by, in a late stage of recovery, she discovers that she no longer feels resentment toward her father. In fact, she can hardly remember the event. She has communicated her concerns to her father, and together they have dealt with them in respectful ways. The hard work of recovery has paid off: safety, predictability, and consistency are now the norm. For a group of individuals who have lived on the edge for years, this feels good.

At times the individuals and the family as a whole must recommit to recovery in order to take it deeper. A friend may ask, "Why do you still go to those meetings after being sober twenty-six years?" Then, we recommit ourselves and may reply, "To make sure I stay sober. I owe this to my family and to myself and my recovery program." Listen to Ruth, who describes how she recommits herself in her thirty-six-year marriage:

> You don't think I know Ed? I know everything about him, what all his little movements mean. I know his body as well as I know my own, yet he still continues to surprise me. Someone asked me how we stay so close after all these years. I don't know, but I do know that we continue the little ways we love. We stare into each other's eyes regularly, we tease and laugh a lot, we make love a lot, we read to each other, and we always hold hands at the movies. All of these things we've done a thousand times before, but we fight to do them with as much love and passion as we did the first

time, knowing that one of these times will be the last. I've often thought if Ed dies, how strange it would be to go to a movie and not have his hand to hold. What would I do with my hands?

## Spiritual Principles Most Helpful in Late Recovery

Spiritual principles have a hierarchy, and some can't be developed and practiced until others have been mastered. The principles of harmony, balance, service, and community involvement in later recovery fall into this category. They can be experienced daily only after others occur in early and middle recovery.

### Harmony and Balance

Harmony helps us see that everything and everyone have their place. When each of us accepts our place and then works to be excellent within it, harmony is created. It can be as simple as accepting our addiction and then working to arrest the disease. Harmony is about order and a respect for that order. Sobriety is a kind of psychological order, especially after an addict who has created havoc in other people's lives finds recovery. The addict will quickly observe how much more harmonious her world is once she can perceive it with eyes not bloodshot from a hangover. Another person, spouse, or family member who tries to control the very course of addiction will quickly experience some unnatural consequences. Being in harmony with others and our environment means we recognize our limits and don't try to shout back a storm, whether it is a real or psychological storm caused by an addict.

To recover from an illness that is, in part, spiritual in nature, we must accept that this order is not made by humans or controlled and directed by someone. To regain spiritual order and harmony, we must reflect and listen for the small quiet voice of the Divine and then do what it says.

When head and heart live within a mutual and honorable relationship, internal harmony is created. Family harmony is not created by everyone agreeing, but occurs when all share an equal place at the table. Each is heard and respected. Each puts aside ego and defers to things that have more importance than self, such as the spirit and things that feed the spirit.

The goal is balance, whether stated or not. Balance is about each person making decisions based on what is best for the relationship. In a balanced relationship the recovering addict meets recovering co-addict and each is seen as equal and needed. You might stay home with the kids so your wife can get to her meeting, and she leaves her meeting five minutes early so you can get to yours. Balance tries to produce a harmonious relationship where members work together, each side respecting the needs and realities of the other. In a family or active addiction many sacrifices are required for the needs of the addict. For example, when a brother gets thrown in jail for drinking and driving, everyone else must set aside their own plans and drive two hundred miles to bail him out of jail. The entire family experiences an ugly weekend. Balance can never be achieved in such an environment. In the recovering family, balance comes from the humility that each family member has gained. Each member truly sees how important he or she is in creating a healthy and loving family.

### Service and Community

Two important principles developed in later recovery are service and community. Service is about how one walks in the world. Service is as much an attitude as it is an activity. Service makes us givers, not just takers. Service for others means seeing a task that needs doing and doing it. If papers need to be put in the basket, you put them in the basket. When the dishwasher needs to be unloaded, you unload it. When the lawn needs to be raked, you start raking. And when these tasks are done, you don't require a parade to honor your accomplishments. Pride in helping out is enough. This kind of service is quite different from the days of addiction where the goal was to see how little one could do. By this time in recovery, service enriches the doer more than anyone else. Service feeds the spirit.

In this stage of recovery and love, community is no longer just self, family, or recovery group. Community means the larger world. Often recovering addicts and families restrict themselves by living in small recovery communities. This is fine for a time. In later recovery, however, people need to step out into the larger community. Your recovery family might start a tradition to serve Thanksgiving dinners to the homeless, volunteer to pick up trash on a local highway, help build houses for Habit for Humanity, or contribute your services to a hospice program in your community.

In the last stage of recovery, shame lifts and a new sense of freedom and confidence appears. The world doesn't seem like such a scary place. For years, your community may have contributed to your recovery in unnoticeable ways. It may have funded the house in which your recovery meetings are hosted; social services might have rescued you once or twice in the past; teachers may have sheltered or given your addicted teens rides home; or the neighborhood police may have shown special understanding when addiction was rampant in your home. Ned's story demonstrates how things like voting in neighborhood elections are often ignored by practicing addicts or angry co-addicts:

> I now vote. I love to vote. Each time I step behind the curtains and make my marks, I walk away feeling complete. This is part of my recovery. I not only vote, but I volunteer down at the food shelf, lifting boxes and stacking canned goods. I've noticed that after voting or doing volunteer work, my whining decreases for a day or two. It feels so much better when I can step outside of my ego and be a member of a community. I'm what is called a good citizen and I feel happy because of it.

By now, we understand that family recovery is a process, a journey, not a single event or destination. It starts with honesty and the admission that something is terribly wrong, namely addiction. Recovery means sitting in meetings, with families like the Jensens, whose story begins each part of this book, and working to be tolerant, honest, and open to strangers who share a critically important experience with you. It involves sitting with your family members and having the courage to listen as they tell you all the horrible things you've done—not because you need to hear them, but because they need to tell you. Wives need to get mad about promises not kept; husbands need to mourn the loss of their spouses; children need to cry about missed birthdays and drunken fights that kept them up at night. Addicts need to learn that addiction is an illness that affects the entire family.

This recovery isn't confined to four weeks in treatment, a number of months in a Twelve Step recovery group, or a process of three stages that ends in bliss. No, recovery is lifelong. It may take a lifetime to learn how to bite your tongue when you feel ugly and mean; to open your mouth when a thank you or a kind, supportive word is needed; and to open your heart and especially your ears and mind to others. We don't finish treatment and suddenly begin to hear the quiet voice of the Divine.

Continuous discipline, service to others in our communities, and good communication with our family members will bring many rewards to our recovery.

Recovery is about healing deep, ugly wounds—wounds of the heart and wounds of the spirit. Recovery is about living a life of honesty and gratitude, by learning how, on a daily basis, to place principles before personality. When the Twelfth Step of Alcoholics Anonymous asks us to "practice these principles in all our affairs," we know that means at work or school, not just in our recovery circles. We go to teacher-parent conferences instead of watching Monday Night Football. It might mean staying up a little late to help a son with his homework or kindly sitting your daughter down and asking her why she took the hair trimmers and shaved the kitten. Yes, you'll experience defeats, losses, and failures, but if you and your family separately and together work at recovery, your tragedies and sorrows will be transformed into joy and hope, just as your addiction and co-addiction were transformed into the peace and serenity called recovery.

# Summary of Phase 3

## LATE RECOVERY

| | |
|---|---|
| **Tasks:** | Continue recommitment to something that members know backward and forward. Allow understanding of recovery to deepen.<br><br>Put old resentments to rest.<br><br>Step out into the larger community—become first-class citizens again. |
| **Changes in Family Interaction Patterns:** | The past is allowed to be the past—resentments rise to the surface and are resolved.<br><br>Family members actively allow themselves to be interdependent on each other.<br><br>The family is reformed around principles of betterment and a reestablished belief and practice of intimacy. Formless love is transformed into creative love.<br><br>The family is able to be both short- and long-term focused because the future isn't scary anymore.<br><br>Family members are able to actively listen—they're able to hear the content, hear the feeling in the content, and hear the history embedded in the content. |
| **Other Characteristics:** | There is continued respect for the power of the illness of addiction. |

Fig. 16

## The Twelve Steps of Alcoholics Anonymous*

1. We admitted we were powerless over alcohol—that our lives had become unmanageable.

2. Came to believe that a Power greater than ourselves could restore us to sanity.

3. Made a decision to turn our will and our lives over to the care of God *as we understood Him*.

4. Made a searching and fearless moral inventory of ourselves.

5. Admitted to God, to ourselves, and to another human being the exact nature of our wrongs.

6. Were entirely ready to have God remove all these defects of character.

7. Humbly asked Him to remove our shortcomings.

8. Made a list of all persons we had harmed, and became willing to make amends to them all.

9. Made direct amends to such people wherever possible, except when to do so would injure them or others.

10. Continued to take personal inventory and when we were wrong promptly admitted it.

11. Sought through prayer and meditation to improve our conscious contact with God *as we understood Him*, praying only for knowledge of His will for us and the power to carry that out.

12. Having had a spiritual awakening as the result of these steps, we tried to carry this message to alcoholics, and to practice these principles in all our affairs.

---

* The Twelve Steps of AA are taken from *Alcoholics Anonymous*, 3d ed., published by AA World Services, Inc., New York, N.Y., 59–60. Reprinted with permission of AA World Services, Inc. (See editor's note on copyright page.)

## Works Cited

*Alcoholics Anonymous: The Story of How Many Thousands of Men and Women Have Recovered from Alcoholism.* 3d ed. New York: Alcoholics Anonymous World Services, 1976.

Becker, Ernest. *Escape from Evil.* New York: The Free Press, 1975.

Bowlby, John. *A Secure Base: Parent-Child Attachment and Healthy Human Development.* New York: Basic Books, 1990.

Covey, Stephen R. *The 7 Habits of Highly Effective People.* New York: Simon and Schuster, 1990.

Erikson, Erik H. *The Life Cycle Completed.* New York: Norton, 1985.

Frankl, Viktor E. *Man's Search for Meaning.* New York: Washington Square Press, 1959.

Fromm, Erich. *The Art of Loving.* New York: Harper and Row, 1956.

Gibran, Kahlil. *Spiritual Sayings of Kahlil Gibran.* Translated and edited by Anthony Rizcallah Ferris. New York: Bantam Books, 1962.

MacIntyre, Alasdair. *After Virtue: A Study in Moral Theory.* South Bend, Ind.: University of Notre Dame Press, 1997.

May, Rollo. *Power and Innocence: A Search for the Sources of Violence.* New York: Dell Publishing, 1972.

*Twenty-Four Hours a Day.* Center City, Minn.: Hazelden, 1954.

Van der Kolk, Bessel A., Alexander C. McFarlane, and Lars Weisaeth. *Traumatic Stress: The Effects of Overwhelming Experience on Mind, Body, and Society.* New York: Guilford Press, 1996.

Werner, Emmy, and Ruth S. Smith. *Vulnerable but Invincible: A Longitudinal Study of Resilient Children and Youth.* New York: Adams Bannister Cox Publishers, 1989.

# Index

## About the Author

Craig Nakken, M.S.W., L.I.C.S.W., L.M.F.T., is a lecturer, trainer, and family therapist who, for over twenty years, has specialized in the treatment of addictions and in counseling couples. He has a private practice in Saint Paul, Minnesota. He speaks and trains professionals, nationally and internationally, on the topics of addiction, family, and principle-centered therapy. He is the author of the best selling book *The Addictive Personality* and other related publications.